ENGAGEMENT WITH KNAVERY

Engagement with Knavery

POINT OF VIEW IN

Richard III, The Jew of Malta, Volpone,

AND *The Revenger's Tragedy*

Robert C. Jones

Duke University Press   Durham 1986

©1986 Duke University Press
All rights reserved
Printed in the United States of America
on acid-free paper
Library of Congress Cataloging in Publication Data
appear on the last page of this book
Grateful acknowledgment is made to *Renaissance Drama*
for permission to include in the Introduction material
from my article, "Dangerous Sport: The Audience's Engagement
with Vice in the Moral Interludes," *Renaissance
Drama* n.s. 6 (1973): 45–64.

For my Parents
Richard H. Jones
and
Alyce E. Jones

Contents

Acknowledgments

Among those who helped me with this book in various ways, I would first like to thank Mari Riess Jones, who gave me support of every important kind throughout its composition. Students in both undergraduate and graduate classes at Ohio State University have, over the past several years, confirmed my belief that questions about point of view open the way toward a fuller understanding and enjoyment of these plays and others. Professors James L. Battersby, John B. Gabel, and Rolf Soellner, all colleagues at Ohio State, read a completed draft of my manuscript and offered encouraging words and instructive criticism. Lester A. Beaurline and Michael E. Mooney suggested important revisions that substantially improved what I had supposed might already be a finished version. Cartha Williams, through the wizardry of the word processor, prepared the final manuscript with amazing skill and speed. Joanne Ferguson, Editor-in-Chief at Duke University Press, has been most helpful and gracious from first to last. Finally, I would like to thank the Center for Medieval and Renaissance Studies at Ohio State for supporting Kathy L. Greenwood as my research associate in 1980–81, and Kathy herself for her invaluable collaboration.

ENGAGEMENT WITH KNAVERY

Introduction

IN THE HANDS OF KNAVES

Anatomical studies probably do not provide much hard data to support young Horatio's proposition, in *The First Part of Hieronimo,* that "knaves longer reaches have than honest men" (3.112). The four plays to be discussed here, however, could be offered as illustrations for such a thesis. The knavish heroes featured in the titles of *Richard III, The Jew of Malta, Volpone,* and *The Revenger's Tragedy* are given a commanding "reach" not only over the action of their respective plays, but over their audiences' view of that action as well. Each serves as the introductory "presenter" and primary contriver of the play we in the audience have come to see. Each shares the fun he has as a "playmaker" with us and thus draws on our natural disposition as theatergoers to appreciate his handiwork with him. The degrees to which we are actually engaged into the sport of these crafty schemers—villains, all—vary a good deal, and the interest of what follows here lies largely in a close examination of the ways in which their efforts to involve us in their knavish points of view succeed or fail. But in each case, our experience of the play is focused so intensely through our responses to the presiding schemer that it is fair to say that we in the audience are, as is so much of what happens onstage, "in the hands of knaves."[1]

Since my argument asserts that these four plays and their heroes make especially interesting use of their audiences' "point of view," some explanation of my attempt to use this and kindred terms as viable tools of dramatic criticism is in order here. I trust that most readers will agree with me that Scholes and Kellogg are rather too stingy when they fence off "the problem of point of view" as "narrative art's own problem, one that it does not share with lyric or dramatic literature."[2] Granted that not even the most insistent chorus can control our view of a presented dramatic action as the narrator who filters our entire experience of a novel through his selective voice can; still, the ways in which our angle of vision is aligned with or distinguished from those of the various participants in a play and the consequences of such alignments for our sense of the play we are watching offer a "problem" of genuine interest to the student (as well as the writer) of drama; and that problem (though I would prefer a term that smiled more invitingly toward our inquiry) surely concerns us with point of view, or perspective. In fact, the twofold implications of these terms make them especially appropriate for my purposes. On the one hand, they emphasize the actual spectator in the theater and the activity of *watching* the performance taking place. In this sense, "point of view" more literally describes an audience's experience of a play than it does a reader's experience of a novel. At the same time, like perspective, point of view suggests the attitude we adopt toward the action we watch and toward the characters who perform it for us. It is precisely that complex activity, the process of forming a particular attitude toward the characters acting before us, that I want to trace as accurately as I can.

Fundamental to the question of dramatic perspective is the relative elevation and comprehensiveness that normally distinguish the audience's view of the whole action from that of any given participant in it. Lear suggests this distinction poignantly through his fragile disregard of it when he tries to raise his blessed reunion with Cordelia above the tragic action that inevitably contains it:

> So we'll live,
> And pray, and sing, and tell old tales, and laugh
> At gilded butterflies, and hear poor rogues
> Talk of court news; and we'll talk with them too—
> Who loses and who wins; who's in, who's out—

And take upon's the mystery of things
As if we were God's spies.
(5.2.11–17)

Only as spectators at a play are we afforded something like the secure elevation and penetrating vision that Lear imagines, "as if we were God's spies." If even as an audience our perspective may be limited—if we sometimes know less than certain characters, and if plays vary in the degree of foreknowledge they allow us and the kinds of "mysteries" with which they may leave us—it is nevertheless true that by the end of the play we have usually seen things more completely and more distinctly than we are able to do outside the theater or than the characters who come and go are able to do within the play itself.

That they come and go while we watch them all is a crucial factor distinguishing our larger view from their limited perspectives, of course. But even characters who see what we see may be most notable for their failure to understand as we do and for the consequent disparity between their view of the action and ours. The result is warm comedy in such a case as *The Knight of the Burning Pestle's* wonderfully naive frame audience. Perhaps a fuller illustration of the uses of disparate perspectives may be found, however, in the darker instance of Kyd's *Spanish Tragedy,* where the limited and distorted views of the participants contribute so largely to the catastrophe, and where the concentric onstage audiences to that catastrophe manage, at best, only a partial understanding of what they see. From our comprehensive vantage point, we see Lorenzo's murderous plot working in the fatal gap between the well-meaning but short-sighted elders of the court on the one hand, who suppose the action is progressing toward a happy nuptial conclusion, and, on the other, a revenge-bound Hieronimo who sees more feelingly than the King and his party, but whose painful vision distorts the complex world around him into a uniformly tragic and "darksome" place (3.11.16 [63]). When Hieronimo at last tries to express and to relieve that vision through the bloody vengeance of his final show—staged, fittingly, in "a mere confusion" of "sundry languages"—he can only stop the questions of his persistently noncomprehending courtly audience by biting out his tongue and stabbing himself to death. That he also stabs the Duke of Castile, whom he has suspected of complicity in Lorenzo's "device" but whom we know to be innocent (3.14.117), adds to our sense of tragic noncommunication in a world where no "actor" is afforded an audience's overview. Andrea's ghost and his sometimes sleepy guide, Revenge, have shared our overview all along, of course; but their smug response to the promised end ("Ay, these were spectacles to please my soul" [4.5.12]) and their narrowly partisan judgments must seem shockingly insufficient to any audience capable of feeling pain and loss as Hieronimo has finally made the bereaved King and Viceroy feel them. The difference, therefore, between our perspective and that of this onstage frame-audience is more a matter of *how* we are made to see and feel than of *what* we see and know.

If *The Spanish Tragedy* makes particularly meaningful use of the fundamental disparity between the audience's privileged vantage point and the limited views of its characters, other plays, of course, gain interest through characters who share our superior perspective on the action. That interest is likely to be provoked less by tiresomely right-minded counterparts to the choral frame of Andrea and Revenge (by Jonson's Cordatus, for example, who explains just what we should think about *Every Man Out of His Humour*) than by actual participants whose wit or fortune gives them, for the moment at least, something like our advantage over their onstage fellows or dupes. "Like a demi-god here sit I in the sky, / And wretched fools' secrets heedfully o'er-eye," crows Berowne in *Love's Labor's Lost*; and, until he slips from his perch and lands ignominiously as one of "four woodcocks in a dish," we enjoy the exposure of those secrets all the more because Berowne enjoys them with us (4.3.74–77). Similar situations are a staple of English Renaissance drama, and though hierarchies of awareness add interest to plays in every theatrical mode, the soliloquies and asides that facilitate our appreciation of them on Shakespeare's open stage make them especially effective there.[3]

Direct communication with the audience through asides and soliloquies also obviously has a major effect on our engagement with certain characters and detachment from others, and can serve to alter our relationship with the same character at different points in the play.[4] "Engagement" and "detachment" are rather more difficult terms — or refer to processes more difficult to demonstrate with precision — than "point of view," "perspective," and "level of awareness," though all five terms are inevitably related to one another. A character whose heightened level of awareness gives him an advantage we share over his fellows has a natural potential to engage us into his point of view and detach us from theirs; but the two processes need not coincide, especially when our feelings are deeply committed to the "ignorant" party. We may see with the more knowing Edgar but feel deeply engaged with the mistaken Lear when "Poor Tom's" disguise gives way in a choral aside to the tears that mar his counterfeiting (3.6.59–60). Or, in a more radical division, we share Iago's level of awareness and Othello's anguish. But these are "heavy matters," and my confidence in accurate measurements of such deeply felt engagement is slight. I can, however, clarify the sort of work I will and will not expect these terms to do here, and my reasons for preferring them to other ways of describing our relationship to the characters onstage.[5]

For one thing, the nature of my four knaves allows my analysis of our engagement with them to avoid most of the implications of subjective emotional involvement or felt kinship that such terms as "sympathy," "empathy," or "identification" inevitably carry with them. Whatever attraction these four schemers hold for us has little to do with sympathy or kinship. And to argue, as I do, that we are engaged into Richard's point of view is not in the least to suggest that we identify with him. His monstrous appearance, of which he makes so much, naturally works to preclude such identification, and the fact that he is a virtual grotesque may actually make it easier to enjoy his villainous fun without seeing ourselves in his image. His grotesqueness is, in fact, a trait that Richard shares in one way or another with many other disreputable knaves who invite our participation in their mischief — Diccon the Bedlam in *Gammer Gurton's Needle*, Marston's Cocledemoy, and the alien, bottle-nosed Barabas, to name a few. It is interesting to note, in this regard, how much less willing critics have been to acknowledge any engagement in the professedly more upright Vindice's vengeance than in the frank villainy of the malicious and malformed Richard. In any case, the distinction between "identification" as it is commonly understood and engagement in a character's point of view should be kept in mind throughout my discussion. We can share a knave's enjoyment of his own sport at a foolish victim's expense without likening ourselves to him.[6]

The suggestion I have just made that we may allow ourselves to share such fun — especially if it involves actions we would ordinarily feel bound to condemn — more openly with a grotesque knave than with an apparently "normal" character is one that bristles with psychological implications, most of which are beyond my ken. Having ventured so far, I would like now to draw back from speculations that might only muddle my argument. To speak of engagement or detachment as I do is, of course, inevitably to imply some sort of psychological transaction between the audience and the character (or actor). It implies less about the psychological nature of that transaction, however, than such terms as empathy or identification would, and, as I have indicated, that suits my endeavor here. I want to show how the dramatist uses his theatrical art to draw us into or distance us from a given character's viewpoint, and I will try to make my argument stand firmly on such demonstration rather than on assumptions about the psychology of the audience. Psychological theories or assumptions have often openly informed statements about what I am calling our engagement with these knaves:

> Although we may feel uneasy about it, our virtuous superego is lulled, and the naked id awakes to vicarious enjoyment of Richard's virtuosity in villainy.[7]

> Richard's ability to rise above the necessities of compromise must fascinate all those who feel the burden of apparently inescapable decorum and constraint that civilization imposes on our basic instincts. His career allows us an initially triumphant indulgence in vicious wish-fulfillment of a kind that was unrecognized by Aristotle, yet is socially purgative in his sense.[8]

If we reserve most of our scorn for the three birds of prey, if we laugh *at* them and *with* Volpone and Mosca during most of the action, it is not only because Corvino, Voltore, and Corbaccio are so repellent, but because Volpone and Mosca act out with such marvellous aplomb our own secret craving to dominate others. We really want to see them get away with it, but Jonson will not indulge us that far.[9]

Oedipal longings and hatreds are presumably universal; the difference is that Vindice acts out these impulses while most of humanity succeeds either in repressing them or in mastering them. . . . If the play does disturb, trouble, or frighten us (and I think many of us respond this way), then we had better acknowledge that *The Revenger's Tragedy* makes us recognize that the crimes we dread the most (incest, parricide, matricide, and regicide) are those that are unconsciously the ones we find the most attractive.[10]

However valid these assertions may be, I have focused my own analysis on the plays' art rather than on the viewers' nature. If doing so limits the explanatory range of my discussion to one side of the theatrical transaction, I hope that it also strengthens the demonstrative force of the argument concentrated on that side. As I suggested above, any such argument would be seriously complicated by characters who make strong demands on our compassion. My discussion, however, features characters who play more to our wit than on our deeper feelings; and where wit and sport dominate, engagement and detachment are likely to be more closely aligned with levels of awareness and more surely demonstrable.

"Wit" and "sport" bring us naturally to our primary subject of knavery. But before describing that subject in more detail, I should acknowledge two further characteristics of my approach to it in the chapters that follow. It should be clear, for one thing, that the understanding my readings aim at has more to do with the experience of each play as it confronts its audience than with a "meaning" or "theme" that might be extracted from it by studying its verbal or structural patterns or its historical context.[11] I am not thereby disclaiming any interest in what a play makes us think. Rather, I am asserting my primary interest in *how* it makes us see, feel, and think as we watch and respond to its characters in action, and how our attitude toward what they say and do is made to correspond with or differ from theirs. Pursuing such questions involves, as an almost inevitable corollary, the habit of referring to the posited audience as "we" or "us," a habit I have already indulged in this Introduction. I am aware that this practice is by no means uncommon, but its general addictiveness will scarcely persuade skeptics of its value or validity.[12] I use the first person plural throughout frankly as a fiction. I can at least claim with Sidney's poet, then, that I can "scarcely be a liar," since I do not propose that this fictive audience ever actually attended one of these plays in some ideal mixture of groundling flesh and noble blood. What I do propose is that the audience I speak of in each case is not so much my creation as the play's, that each play "implies" an audience to appreciate it in its own terms.[13] By yoking my imagination as tightly as possible to the matter in hand, then, and attempting to follow its lead, I part company with Sidney's free-ranging poet and try to obey one Baconian precept even while I am violating another by lingering in the theater. But attending closely to these plays does not reveal a highly particularized image of the spectator who might properly enjoy each of them. If each implies specific responses throughout, none addresses itself exclusively to a select or special audience—to the "very fine Heliconian gallants" to whom Cocledemoy appeals in the epilogue of *The Dutch Courtesan*, for example, or to the "spectators or hearers at the Hope on the Bankside in the county of Surrey" on "the one and thirtieth day of October, 1614" with whom the author of *Bartholomew Fair* struck an agreement. Except for *The Jew of Malta's* clear indication that its professedly Christian audience would normally enjoy the sport of Jew-baiting, the basic traits that these plays attribute to their audiences and that are relevant to my argument are universal enough to fit any of "us," be "we" Elizabethan or modern. All four works imply (and I posit along with them) an audience that has come to enjoy a play and appreciate the theatrics that make it lively and an audience that, in thinking rather better than worse of itself, would ordinarily both disapprove of such immoral and antisocial actions as murder and theft and prefer to align itself with wit rather than folly when the two meet onstage. No particular characteristics of the audience beyond these, I think, are essential to my argument at any point.

The inherent tension between the "normal" responses on which these plays do rely lends a special interest to our engagement with knavery in them, since our natural attraction as an audience to the playful spirit of wit is commanded in each case by a knave who should also provoke our customary disapproval of malicious crimes. The term "knave," as it applies to each of these schemers, includes a full measure of villainy along with its mischievous wit. All four plays involve us at different points in both appreciation and condemnation of their knavish heroes, since each ends with the downfall and punishment of the villain whose sport we have been made to enjoy and whose own view of the action we are sometimes invited to share.[14]

The contradictory attitudes these knaves almost inevitably provoke in us make our relationship with them, or the play's use of our point of view toward them, a more complex process than it would be in the cases of their near kindred on either side, the blameless wits who entertain us in many comedies and the joyless or foolish villains whose deeds we readily condemn in various tragedies. There is little to inhibit our delight in the pure "sport alone" that Puck enjoys at the expense of foolish mortals whom we can watch along with him from our temporary elevation as "demi-gods" in the audience (though *A Midsummer Night's Dream* may remind us, as well, of our kinship to those mortals and suggest that Puck's is not the most penetrating view of their woes [3.2.119]). And the carefully laundered fun of the merry wives of Windsor—"admirable pleasures and fery honest knaveries" (4.4.78–79)—is, like that of their wholesome predecessor Dame Christian Custance in *Ralph Roister Doister*, so spotlessly clean that the most fastidious audience need feel no qualms about sharing it. If the comedy approves their goals, rakish gallants who would never be allowed to enter Dame Custance's prim parlor can nonetheless engage us in their schemes without troubling our consciences, as can less respectable pranksters whose fun proves no more harmful than Diccon's in *Gammer Gurton's Needle* or who can disclaim knavery's villainous aims as freely as does Marston's Cocledemoy: "No knave, worshipful friend, no knave; for observe, honest Cocledemoy restores whatsoever he has got, to make you know that whatsoe'er he has done has been only *euphoniae gratia*—for wit's sake. . . . All has been done for emphasis of wit, my fine boy, my worshipful friends" (*The Dutch Courtesan*, 5.3.132–37). And a tricky servant of Brainworm's benign sort gains our ready applause, along with Justice Clement's pardon, "for the wit o' the offense" (*Every Man in His Humour*, 5.3.113).

On the other hand, the absence of this puckish spirit of sheer, mischievous fun can leave us totally detached from a villain who has no other capacity to involve us (as Macbeth surely does involve us) in his problems. Paradoxically, the more detached a knave can remain from the self-serving goals of his scheme—the more, that is, he approximates the spirit of Puck's "sport alone" as he plays on his victims—the more engaged we are likely to be in his fun and his point of view. None of the four knaves who are the principals in this book could fairly claim with Cocledemoy that "whatsoe'er he has done has been only *euphoniae gratia*— for wit's sake"; but they engage us insofar as they catch us up in their "emphasis of wit." If Volpone sometimes works too hard at his sport, he nonetheless suggests what makes a knave winning for us when he says that he glories "more in the cunning purchase" of his wealth "than in the glad possession" (1.1.30–32).[15]

Successful knaves customarily invite our participation in their fun by sharing it with us through soliloquies and asides that confirm the mutual superiority of our awareness over their hapless dupes. There is, however, nothing intrinsically winning about confidentiality. A villain's soliloquy, even when it provides our heightened overview of the action, can as easily make us abhor or oppose him as enjoy him. To cite a rather crude example, the soliloquy with which Selimus introduces himself to us in the play that bears his name, though it "unmasks" his Machiavellian plans "to set barrels of blood abroach, / And seeke with sword whole kingdomes to displace," does nothing whatsoever to engage us with the schemer because he himself has none of the knavish zest for mischief and none of the creative wit that would turn his scheme into "sport" for his amusement and ours. Instead, he simply exposes his atrocious villainy to us, showing himself to us as "the perfect picture of right tyrannie" (2.231–382). As Richard III correctly observes at a critical moment in his own villainous career, "None are for me / That look into me with considerate eyes" (4.2.29–30). When a villain's soliloquy simply invites us to look into him and consider his villainy, it speaks to our normal judgment of such crimes without engaging our natural theatrical attraction to playful wit and creative dramatic art. The contrast between Selimus's dour self-portrait and Richard's own early soliloquies illustrates the clear distinction between engaging knavery and exposed villainy. Richard is cleverly showing off (not just showing) his villainy in those speeches. Showing off *can* be dangerous, of course. A villain who boasts foolishly of his own cleverness subverts any potential command he might have over our point of view, even more surely than a straight expositor like Selimus, by making himself the comic target of our derision, as Piero does with his "braggart passion" in the opening scene of Marston's *Antonio's Revenge*. Such overweening self-satisfaction is an occupational hazard even for truly witty knaves, as we shall see.

It is, then, the combination of puckish sport and malicious crime that distinguishes the knave from either honest wits on the one hand or solemn villains on the other and complicates our relationship with him in the plays to be discussed here. Perhaps the closest analogue to that relationship is the one that was carried on between the Vice in the moral interludes and the audiences he entertained virtually up to the time when Shakespeare and Marlowe conceived their knavish heroes. The fact that it is a morality play's explicit business to make us reject the Vice, who provides its primary theatrical attraction for us, brings the inherent complication in our relationship with its engaging "knave" openly to the surface, more so than need be the case in the less overtly didactic plays we will be considering. I have tried to show elsewhere how morality dramatists use the open interactions between their antic Vices and their audiences to reinforce rather than subvert the doctrine of their plays—how audiences are actually made to act out their rejection of the Vice.[16] A brief review here of that characteristic process in the moralities may provide a useful comparative context for my more detailed studies of the later knaves who both resemble the Vice and differ from him in important respects.

The potential conflict between didactic purpose and theatrical engagement in the morality plays is nicely illustrated by C. L. Barber's description of festive comedy's prevailing mood: "Behind the laughter at the butts there is always a sense of solidarity about pleasure, a communion embracing the merry-makers in the play and the audience, who have gone on holiday in going to a comedy."[17] It is not hard to imagine something very like this experience taking place at the performance of moral interludes that include large measures of the sort of merrymaking that almost always turns at some point on laughter at the butt of a joke or trick—laughter in which the audience is openly invited to join by the merry prankster who shares his superior level of awareness with us. But if this communal spirit actually united the merrymakers onstage and in the audience with no counterforce to break the union, it would be absolutely subversive to the moral purpose of the plays, since the tricksters onstage are always the chief representatives of vice (or "the Vice"), and the poor dupe at whom we are asked to laugh is often the figure of mankind. In other words, insofar as the vices' mirth is theatrically successful in Barber's terms, the audience is put in the position of laughing at the representation of its own ruin.

This problem of the audience's theatrical engagement with vicious sport might seem especially acute in those later moralities where the presiding Vice presents and directs most of the action, very much in the manner of the knaves we will be focusing on. Ulpian Fulwell's *Like Will to Like* (1568), which fits this description precisely, also shows how the sort of communion of merrymakers that Barber speaks of is purposefully averted in these interludes. As in some other later moralities, the Vice's dupes at whom we laugh in Fulwell's play are not representatives of mankind in general but types of folly and roguery from which we are meant to dissociate ourselves. The butts of the Vice's jokes are therefore the deserving objects of our derision. But the basic problem remains the same. We may be quite properly laughing at Tom Tosspot or Cuthbert Cutpurse, but if we are laughing altogether *with* the Vice, Nichol Newfangle, as he snares his victims into the Devil's party, we are sharing a point of view that is perilous for us according to the play's morality. Fulwell turns this danger to our advantage by making the spirit we might share with Newfangle, or our possible kinship with him, an object of satire, with Newfangle himself acting as the satirist in his interactions with us. That is, much of the fun he has with us is precisely on the subject of our likeness to him, playing on the proverb that gives this interlude its title. He rubs our noses in our presumed alliance with him in a way that may make us laugh, but we must laugh self-consciously, rejecting his innuendoes for our own sakes and thereby rejecting him. Here is how it works.

After a prologue has explained the lesson of the play's title, Nichol bounds in, laughing jauntily, and starts things off by tossing down a playing card in front of one of us (it is, apparently visibly, the knave of clubs). His first few lines explicate the business:

> Ha, ha, ha, ha! now like unto like: it will be none other,
> Stoop, gentle knave, and take up your brother.
> Why, is it so? and is it even so indeed?
> Why then may I say God send us good speed!
> And is every one here so greatly unkind,
> That I am no sooner out of sight, but quite out of mind?
> Marry, this will make a man even weep for woe,
> That on such a sudden no man will let me know,
> Sith men be so dangerous now at this day:
> Yet are women kind worms, I dare well say.
> How say you woman? you that stand in the angle,
> Were you never acquainted with Nichol Newfangle?
> Then I see Nichol Newfangle is quite forgot,
> Yet you will know me anon, I dare jeopard a groat.
> Nichol Newfangle is my name, do you not me know?
> My whole education to you I shall show.[18]

Notice here that Nichol's fun comes in the form of taunts that play satirically on our imputed friendship with him; and Nichol's lines make clear that our response to his gibes, however amused we may be, must involve embarrassed rejection of the familiar advances and insinuations of our likeness to him. So the dramatist, in this fairly simple and direct way, turns his Vice's sport, which is the play's main theatrical attraction, into a means for detaching the audience from the Vice. Though Nichol continues to entertain us, the rest of the play is devoted to reinforcing that rejection through the illustrative examples of the characters onstage who welcome or rebuff his proffered friendship.

This sort of confrontation, in which our theatrical response defines our relationship to the Vice (or vices), is constant throughout the morality plays. From *The Castle of Perseverance* on, we are invited to join company with the vices and thereby prompted to act out our refusal to do so:

> Cum speke wyth Lust and Lykynge belyue
> And hys felaw, yonge Foly.
> Late se whoso wyl vs knowe.
> Whoso wyl drawe to Lykynge and Luste
> And as a fole in Foly ruste,
> On vs to he may truste
> And leuyn louely, I trowe.[19]

Or, turned the other way, the extent of our complicity with the scheming Vice can be satirically pointed up by making us share in a conspiratorial silence with him:

> Peace, peace! she commeth hereby.
> I spoke no word of her, no, not I![20]

Perhaps the most interesting instance of such overt "complicity" occurs in *Mankind* (ca. 1471), a morality that makes especially bold use of our engagement with its comic vices as entertainers. At the midpoint of this play the extent to which we are falling into the very sort of "negligence" against which the pious Mercy had warned us in his opening sermon is dramatized when the festive vices literally stop the show and make us pay them before we get to see their main attraction—the duping of Mankind by that "Fend of helle," Titivillus:

> Ye, go thi wey! We xall gather mony onto,
> Ellys ther xall no man hym se.
> Now gostly to owr purpos, worschypfull souerence,
> We intende to gather mony, yf yt plesse yowr neclygence.[21]
> (ll. 457–60)

This last phrase, whether it be a slip of the tongue, a malapropism, or a direct taunt, points out exactly how our situation can be judged in the play's terms. We are paying to suit the pleasure of our "neclygence."

Once Titivillus comes on, we are put in the position of acting as his confidants and accomplices in his successful deception of Mankind. From the moment he enters, he treats us as admiring potential henchmen whom he is taking under his wing and teaching the tricks of his trade: "Titivillus kan lerne yow many praty thyngys" (l. 572). First he warns us, as insiders, to watch out for *our* belongings as he sends out the other vices, Newguise, Nowadays, and Nought, to plunder our neighbors in the local countryside (ll. 476–524). Then he proudly reveals his scheme against Mankind to us, promising us "goode sport" in his execution of it, and beseeching our conspiratorial silence as he carries it out:

> Ande euer ye dyde, for me kepe now yowr sylence.
> Not a worde, I charge yow, peyn of forty pens.
> A praty game xall be scheude yow or ye go hens.
> Ye may here hym snore; he ys sade aslepe.
> Qwyst! pesse! the Deull ys dede! I xall goo ronde in hys ere.
> (ll. 589–93)

The audience is not likely to take this stage fiend's "ab-homynabull presens" or his bag of tricks very seriously, of course, but that is just the point. We are being caught up in the "sport" of the thing without thinking much about its implications. It is only when the trap is successfully sprung and Mankind has succumbed to Titivillus's deceptive spells that we are brought up suddenly and rudely against the full consequences of this "praty game." The turn comes when Titivillus, having done his business, leaves us abruptly (and no doubt with an abusive gesture). The tone of camaraderie is gone as he points out exactly what he has accomplished:

> Farwell, euerychon! for I haue don my game,
> For I haue brought Mankynde to myscheff and to schame.
> (ll. 605–6)

After Titivillus has departed, the play takes on a new tone. As Mankind awakens with his faith in Mercy entirely broken, the other vices (who have treated us as familiar friends all along) return to welcome him into their company. But they return with a difference. The bawdy songs and raucous pranks with which they have hitherto entertained us have been replaced by bloody murders and the hangman's noose. Newguise staggers on with half a halter around his neck, soon followed by Mischief with the remnants of fetters on his arms. What he has been up to is more than mischief:

> Of murder and manslawter I haue my bely-fyll.
> . . . . .
> I was chenyde by the armys: lo, I haue them here.
> The chenys I brast asundyr and kyllyde the jaylere.
> (ll. 639–43)

Moreover, their demeanor toward us has changed as well. Whereas they had earlier wooed us into sharing their festive spirit, they now shoulder us rudely aside as they come on:

> Make space, for cokkys body sakyrde, make space!
> (l. 612)

> Avante, knawys, lett me go by!
> (l. 636)

> Out of my wey, sers, for drede of fyghtynge!
> (l. 696)

Taking customary advantage of a theater in which players enter and exit through the audience, the play thus alienates us from its vices through their direct interaction with us as well as through our responses to their more starkly (and less comically) exposed viciousness. The remainder of the play confirms that dissociation, and in the aftermath of our experience with these vices, we should be in a fit frame of mind to heed Mercy's concluding exhortation to search our "condycyons wyth dew examinacion" (l. 908).

Few moralities make the audience's experience of the play so fully analogous to the mankind figure's seduction by the vices as *Mankind* does. Even when (and perhaps because) the Vice took over a larger proportion of the action in the later interludes, most dramatists were careful to prod the audience into acting out its dissociation from the Vice early in the play, in the very process of being entertained by him. Nichol Newfangle's opening confrontation is the more common technique. But the point to be stressed here is that all of the morality vices interact with us directly and call open attention to the implications of our responses to them. Thus, when the Vice Inclination in *The Trial of Treasure* becomes the mocker mocked, we not only laugh at him, but are characteristically made conscious of that response and of the fact that it dissociates us from him: "Ye have no pity on me, you, I see by your laughing."[22] Even in such a sophisticated morality as *Mankind*, where our relationship with the vices moves from engagement to detachment in a way that resembles the pattern I will be describing in *Richard III*, our necessary self-consciousness about our actual interactions with the vices sharply distinguishes the earlier dramatist's method from Shakespeare's. The many likenesses between the morality vices and their Elizabethan and Jacobean heirs have prompted recent scholarship to stress the continuity that binds them, a bond that Richard himself is pleased to acknowledge:

> Thus, like the formal Vice, Iniquity,
> I moralize two meanings in one word.[23]
> (3.1.82–83)

But a fundamental distinction between Richard and "the formal Vice" makes the job of tracing the audience's theatrical engagement with or detachment from Shakespeare's villain and his fellow knaves less simple than it is when we are dealing with their morality forebears. Since some of these later knaves are as vicious as Iniquity could ever hope to be, and since they oppose "Virtues" as pure as Richmond and Celia, the distinction is not a moral one but one of theatrical mode. Though the Shakespearean villain and Jonsonian knave make direct appeals to us from the stage, they do not openly interact with us or even overtly acknowledge our responses as an audience, except by way of inviting our applause at the end of a comedy. For all the versatile theatricalism that allows them their explanatory soliloquies and mocking asides, the knaves to be considered here do not jostle us as they enter or exit, do not taunt us about our displayed behavior toward them, and do not invite us to join in their activities as did their earlier counterparts in the moral interludes. In the move from hall to theater, from "place" to stage, the Vice's knavish heirs distance themselves from us to this extent. They still play *to* us, but they do not force us to be participating actors *in* their plays and do not therefore make us self-consciously act out our conspiratorial engagement with them ("Ande euer ye dyde, for me kepe now yowr sylence") or our dissociation from them ("Ye have no pity on me, you, I see, by your laughing"). Consequently, the argument that follows here demands careful analysis of verbal and dramatic gestures subtler than those of the moral interludes, where the audience's responses are written so plainly into the dialogue of the plays themselves.

My distinction between "place" and stage may seem to ignore Robert Weimann's sophisticated and influential argument that the earlier drama's effective interplay between *platea* (the unlocalized "place" or nonrepresentational area where actors could mingle with the audience) and *locus* (a more or less fixed scenic unit within which the represented action "could assume an illusionary character") was in fact incorporated onto Shakespeare's stage. As will be clear by now, I share Weimann's belief that "the actor-audience relationship was not subordinate, but a dynamic and essential element of dramaturgy" in the English Renaissance theater.[24] For Weimann, that relationship involves a special contact between the audience and the self-expressive actor who addresses us directly from his *platea*-oriented proximity to us (as both Nichol and Richard do in their opening speeches) and who, from that perspective, tends to shatter the illusion (in *both* senses, theatrical and ideal) that is represented in the self-contained *locus*-based action. To take a characteristic Shakespearean example, while Silvia and Valentine exchange courtly compliments in *The Two Gentlemen of Verona* (2.1.88 ff.), the clown, Speed, employs asides to

> address the audience in the manner of a chorus; and it is through the choric quality of Speed's comments that a dramatic interplay between the wit of the audience and the

wittiness of the clown is achieved. The resulting laughter, both in the yard and on the scaffold, shares the same perspective toward its object. That object (Silvia's and Valentine's high-flown addresses) is part of the play world, but the perspective of his comic "asides" links the clown with the real world of everyday experience. This involves some contact between the audience and the actor of Speed's part who, as comic chorus, enjoys a level of awareness that is not strictly limited by the play world. The resulting unity of mirth between the audience and the actor-character . . . succeeds in building up a wider comic vision through which the main theme of friendship and courtly love . . . is dramatically controlled and comically evaluated.[25]

This analysis of shared perspectives and levels of awareness, which suggests engagement with one onstage point of view and detachment from another, is very close in kind to much that will follow here, and certain movements and placements of my four knaves can be seen readily enough in Weimann's terms. It would be fair to say, for example, that we become more detached from Richard as he moves from his early *platea*-oriented position near the audience to the *locus*-based throne. Or we could diagram Vindice's vantage point in similar terms as he comments on the courtly procession for us to open *The Revenger's Tragedy*.[26]

On the whole, however, I want to emphasize a distinction between Nichol and Richard that Weimann's thesis minimizes and to point out aspects of the "actor-audience relationship" that sometimes run counter to the natural alignment he posits between *platea*-oriented characters and the spectators. The nature of our engagement with Richard depends partly on the degree to which he remains *within* the self-contained world of the play rather than breaking through it in Nichol's overt manner. And as I have already suggested, Nichol's self-expressive *way* of insisting on direct contact with us can have the effect of forcing our conscious dissociation from him, as well as linking him "with the real world of [our] everyday experience," the link that Weimann would emphasize. This is not to say, of course, that *Richard III* is a "self-contained" or "illusionistic" play in the way that Ibsen's drama attempts to be. Its flexible theatricalism, rather, allows dynamic interaction with the audience without insisting that we reflect on that experience or consciously assess the relationship between our "real world" and the presented dramatic illusion. Of the four plays to be considered here, only *The Jew of Malta* makes such an assessment an important element in our relationship with the presiding knave. In that case, Marlowe stands Weimann's scheme on its head, for it is the audience-oriented Barabas whom we are encouraged to place in a fictive (if scarcely "ideal") play world and the self-contained Ferneze in whom we recognize "the real world of everyday experience." Weimann probably could account for such reversals in his own terms, but any attempt I might make to apply those terms systematically throughout would, I fear, either oversimplify my argument by suggesting alignments that are too schematically neat or overburden it with explanations of every deviation from those alignments.

A similar desire for reasonable clarity and directness has prompted another decision. Since my analyses of our developing view of each play's action are by nature linear and by necessity detailed, I have chosen not to clutter the line or extend the length of the argument by including encounters with previous scholarship in the text of each chapter. By relegating material of this sort mostly to notes, some of which may therefore bulge to unseemly proportions, I leave the pursuit of such byways to the inclination of the reader. I can, however, briefly forecast here some general patterns in the relationship that emerges between my readings of these plays and much of the extant critical work on them.

There is a fundamental distinction between readings that apply an "objective" standard of behavior (often putatively Elizabethan) to the characters and judge them accordingly, on the one hand, and, on the other, my attempt to show how these knaves play to our theatrical engagement or detachment and thereby affect our point of view. Moral (or thematic) judgment and theatrical viewpoint need not, of course, be divided in any given case; the latter may be brought into play directly and explicitly in behalf of the former. In these four cases, however, the differences are often pronounced, and they are clearly represented in conflicting critical arguments about each play.

Studies of *Richard III*, for example, openly reflect the divisive

pull between theatrical attraction and moral judgment that is
intrinsic to the knaves considered in this book. In this respect, as
in others, Richard can serve as a model for the other three,
clarifying the issue by provoking critics to assume extreme
stances on either side of it. These range from the romantic
enthusiasm of Charles Lamb's remark, "I am possessed with an
admiration of the genuine Richard, his genius, and his mounting
spirit," to the moral orthodoxy imposed by Lamb's onetime
editor, E. M. W. Tillyard, who anathematizes Richard as "the
great ulcer of the body politic into which all its impurity is
drained and against which all the members of the body politic
are united."[27] Tillyard's task, as he saw it, was to wrench our
fascinated attention away from "Richard's character in itself" so
that we might recognize "the greater scheme" of retributive
providence to which that character is properly "subservient." It
was not in Tillyard's power, of course, to keep anyone's eyes off
Richard for long. Whatever critics think about him, it is Richard
they think about when they discuss this play. Many, however,
follow Tillyard's lead in attempting first of all to locate Richard
safely within the proper moral or providential perspective, as
Virgil K. Whitaker does when he praises Shakespeare for
"placing the particular action in a context of larger moral
forces."[28] The distinction between such analyses and mine,
clearly, is that they determine what the proper perspective (as
suggested by the entire play and other sources) *is*, and then view
Richard accordingly. M. M. Reese's transition from his account
of the "proper view" to a treatment of Richard's entertaining
sport nicely exposes the priorities of this approach: "Such is the
official Richard; and *having determined our official attitude to
him*, we are free to enjoy his company" (my italics).[29] If we are
primarily concerned to find out what we finally *ought* to think
about Richard, this method may serve, but it does not show (or
even acknowledge), as I attempt to do, how the play directs our
perspective on Richard as we watch it and how we are invited to
"enjoy his company" *before* the "official attitude" gains any
dramatic force.

Again, I am not opposing moral readings of this or any other
play per se, but rather offering an alternative to the prior
assumptions that frequently guide such readings. As it happens,

I end my reading of *Richard III* very much where the moralists do because I think that this particular play steers us progressively toward that end. The case will alter with *The Jew of Malta* and *The Revenger's Tragedy*, where I believe that "official attitudes" have been imposed more arbitrarily. My approach to all the plays, then, is not so much ideological as theatrical; I try to follow wherever they direct us dramatically and *as* they direct us. For that reason, my reading of *Richard III* differs from skeptical assaults on Tillyard's "official" thesis as much as it does from that thesis itself insofar as the skepticism depends on reflective analysis that could play no part in an audience's progressive experience of a performance. What I am characterizing here as skeptical readings usually stress the moral as well as theatrical shortcomings of those who oppose Richard in the play.[30] Such analyses, though they frequently cite theatrically engaging aspects of Richard's character that are important to my argument as well, inevitably present a more "interesting" view of the play in certain respects than I do, since they posit the complication or subversion of distinctions between Richard and his antagonists that I will argue are clear and absolute. Some, like Wilbur Sanders, provide a full consideration of the historical and political issues that illuminate the dramatized events.[31] But even those skeptical readers who rely more exclusively than Sanders does on evidence from the play itself imply a *considered* reading that scrutinizes lines and actions reflectively in order to derive that evidence, whereas I am trying to follow the clear directives given an audience as it watches and responds to the play in progress. Thus Sanders's fully informed argument will hover over a passage or the whole play with phrases such as "when we recall" or "one has only to pause for a moment to consider"; and A. L. French can select Stanley's role out of the flow of the play and study its implications when so isolated, remarking along the way that "*as we ponder the play, we begin to wonder*" how far Richmond really is presented as an official Tudor hero" (my italics).[32] I would only suggest such a reflective process if the particular sequence under discussion pointedly triggers the audience's "recollection" or prompts us to "pause" and "realize," as happens during those static scenes of reflection that punctuate the action of *Richard III*. Such reflective moments *in* the play overtly express its solid moral overview, I believe, and it is mainly by "pondering the play" at their own discretion that skeptics call that moral overview into question. I am not faulting the method, but simply distinguishing it and its results from mine.[33]

This distinction between methods and goals should be even more apparent when my reading diverges more sharply from critical consensus, as it does with *The Jew of Malta*. This play, once "the standing puzzle of the English stage,"[34] has been resolved into coherence by several studies over the past thirty years, most of which employ thematic analyses to find a consistent moral vision at work throughout Marlowe's bizarre mixtures of tone and substance. Rather than attempting to harmonize the play, my own reading attends instead to the jolting shifts in perspective that its sudden turns force upon an audience. Where our normal expectations are assaulted so violently, coherent thematic and moral interpretation necessarily depends heavily on a reader's considered judgments, comparisons, and pursuit of allusions. The resulting measured assessment is frequently offered as though it were the only significant response addressed by the play. Surely Barabas *is* bad and Abigail *is* good, but our experience of them is scarcely limited to that not very astonishing judgment, however reinforced it might be with references to biblical or other sources. Not many who present learned interpretations of the play openly raise the question of the kind of understanding they address and its relationship to or distance from an audience's experience. Douglas Cole, explicating Barabas's inversion of Job's patience, is exceptionally candid in this regard when he claims that "it does not really matter that this point-for-point contrast may not be dramatically evident to the audience; it reveals, most importantly, the dramatist's *conception* behind the presentation of the character, which is grounded on the complete and consistent inversion of accepted values and virtues."[35] If it is the underlying *conception* we seek, Cole's point may well be granted. Since, however, the effect of the progressive "presentation of the character" on our point of view is my primary concern, then what is "dramatically evident to the audience" is precisely what matters most here.

Having insisted so emphatically on the audience's experience, I must acknowledge that my readings of these four plays *are* "readings" and are products of the study more than of the theater in one important sense. My analyses are based on my understanding of the plays as I believe they are written to be performed more than on my experience of (or research into) actual performances. I have, to be sure, attended performances of these plays whenever possible, learned how to read a play largely from the experience of watching plays, and modified my understanding of a given play according to what I have seen onstage. Nevertheless, I don't consider any single production an ultimate test of my reading, and I continue to test the former by the latter. That may be a risky confession to make as studies of this period's drama become more performance-oriented, but my evenings spent watching Elizabethan plays with Elizabethan scholars convince me that I am scarcely unique in this regard. In any case, even a compelling portrayal of Richard as a more anguished and less playful villain than I understand him to be will not persuade me that I am misreading the lines. It will persuade me, rather, that the actor or director is reading *between* the lines, as Freud said we must do in order to understand the true agony of this character:

> Richard's [opening] soliloquy does not say everything; it merely gives a hint, and leaves us to fill in what it hints at. When we do so, however, the appearance of frivolity vanishes, the bitterness and minuteness with which Richard has depicted his deformity make their full effect, and we clearly perceive the fellow feeling which compels our sympathy even with a villain like him.[36]

Taking Hamlet's assurance that "the players cannot keep counsel; they'll tell all" (3.2.135–36) as a guiding principle, I try to hear and respond to what is *in* Richard's lines, not to "fill in" what may lurk behind them. It is, of course, encouraging to note that what I have seen and read of Richard onstage more often than not confirms my argument that his mischievous wit will engage an audience into sharing his amusement and enjoying his craft with him through much of the play.[37] In the chapters that follow, I will occasionally take note of performances that bear out my reading or—and these seem to me even more telling instances—

performances that alter the text or add stage business to make a character either more or less engaging than I understand him to be. But the primary authority for the performance posited by each of my readings remains the text of the play itself rather than its theater history.

Before letting the knaves take the stage, I should add two more prefatory notes. I have been speaking thus far in general terms that might imply not only generic resemblance but an identical likeness among the four principals to be discussed here. What follows should gain interest, however, at least as much from the differences that emerge as from the likenesses that identify each hero as a knave. I begin with Shakespeare's Richard, who provides a comparatively clear model against which the complexities of the other three knaves and their plays can be usefully set off. Because he does so, previous readings of *Richard III* anticipate the line of my argument about that play rather more closely than is the case with *The Jew of Malta, Volpone,* or *The Revenger's Tragedy.* I hope that what I say about Richard justifies itself by its own interest, but it should also establish a helpful vantage point from which to examine the trickier terrain of the other three plays.

I close my introduction with what may serve as a *caveat lector,* though I would prefer that it be taken as an invitation. The arguments that follow depend on close analysis—sometimes speech by speech, sometimes scene by scene—of each play's unfolding dialogue and action. I know of no other way to demonstrate convincingly how an audience's developing view of the play is aligned with or detached from those of the characters. But I should hasten to add that I do not therefore consider my method a necessary evil to which my argument is reluctantly bound. Instead, I take frank pleasure in the close contact with these knaves and their plays that my discussion of them demands. I have already stated that a play "implies" its audience, as a book implies its readers. The readers implied in the chapters that follow are those who share the pleasure of that contact, whether they agree with the conclusions reached through it or not.

1

Richard III

THE VITAL COCKATRICE

There is no puzzle about the attitude we *should* adopt toward Richard as Shakespeare presents him to us. Not even a mother could approve of him, as the Duchess of York makes painfully clear:

> O my accursèd womb, the bed of death!
> A cockatrice hast thou hatched to the world,
> Whose unavoided eye is murderous.[1]

We should not look at a cockatrice at all. But from our privileged sanctuary in the audience, Shakespeare allows us to meet Richard's eye, to share his knavish high spirits, and then brings us off alive and well and feeling morally intact. Since Richard is a determined villain from beginning to end, our developing relationship with him is more interesting than any development in his character. As we watch him through the play, we follow a neatly plotted course that takes us from engagement with his winning knavery to detachment from his cringing villainy. Though that brief description of our responses through this long play necessarily oversimplifies the case somewhat, it is nonetheless fair to say that we can smile with our knavish villain and then enjoy his downfall without undergoing any very uncomfortable moments of self-examination in the process. Such complacence may be well enough suited to a world so sharply defined as Richard's is by its carefully balanced rhetorical and theatrical gestures into absolute distinctions between good and evil—a world that works, in spite of its plentiful miseries, toward a

happy ending under the providential eye of "that high All-seer."
Other knaves, at work or at play in more problematical theatrical
worlds, may trouble us more. Here, Richard carries whatever
burden of guilt we might have been made to feel away on his own
bunched back and leaves us applauding his saintly successor.[2]

At the beginning, however, the play is all Richard's. He has the
presenter's natural command over our point of view in the
opening scene, and he uses it to draw us into his perspective in
the very process of declaring and demonstrating his outright
villainy.[3] Like other distinctions in this play, that between our
theatrical appreciation and our moral judgment is, throughout
these first few sequences, absolute. There can be no doubt that
the attitude we are made to enjoy here is a vicious one, but we are
made to enjoy it nevertheless. It is not simply that Richard has
our eye and ear—it is what he does with them that engages us
here. As we have seen, a confidential exposition of villainy need
not be intrinsically winning, especially if it invites us to look into
the villain himself "with considerate eyes." But Richard's knavish
spirit is infectious in ways that keep considered judgment in
check for the time being.

We catch that spirit first through Richard's tone. The peace on
earth he describes in his opening lines ought to suit our hearts'
desire, but he converts it into an object of ridicule through his
comic image of Mars turned fop:

> Grim-visaged war hath smoothed his wrinklèd front,
> And now, instead of mounting barbèd steeds
> To fright the souls of fearful adversaries,
> He capers nimbly in a lady's chamber
> To the lascivious pleasing of a lute.

So we find ourselves smiling with him at this "weak piping
time of peace." His mocking tone may not be written so
broadly into the series of antitheses with which this speech (and
the play) begins:

> Now is the winter of our discontent
> Made glorious summer by this son of York;
> . . . . . .

Now are our brows bound with victorious wreaths,
Our bruisèd arms hung up for monuments,
Our stern alarums changed to merry meetings,
Our dreadful marches to delightful measures.

Such perfect harmony should please us in most contexts. But here Richard can work on our feeling, as an audience prepared to watch a play, that this is precisely the *wrong* context for such a speech. We want an action to begin, not end, and what he offers us in these opening lines is, in effect, the epilogue to a happy ending, a signal to applaud and disperse. That will do nicely when Richmond rounds off the play ("Now civil wounds are stopped, peace lives again"), but we are scarcely ready for it *yet*. When, therefore, in the fundamental antithesis of his opening speech, Richard sets himself against the world at peace, the knave's natural theatrical attraction as a playmaker works with particular force:

Plots have I laid, inductions dangerous,
By drunken prophecies, libels, and dreams,
To set my brother Clarence and the king
In deadly hate the one against the other.

We *want* "inductions" rather than conclusions here, and it is Richard alone who will provide the momentum for the play we have come to see.[4]

If we can't help but engage ourselves with Richard's dramatic impulse, however, we needn't associate ourselves consciously with him or his values. This foul-looking creature is avowedly a villain, "subtle, false, and treacherous," who sets out to destroy the "true and just." The movement of the play will ultimately bring our responses as an audience in line with our conventional (and healthy) moral judgments on such a course of action. But if for the moment we can both see the better and enjoy the worse, Richard does nothing to provoke any uncomfortable awareness of that disparity on our part. Theatrical engagement in his knavery is all the easier here since its implications are not exposed for us as they had been in the morality plays. Richard neither hails us as his colleagues in the manner of Nichol Newfangle nor solicits our conspiratorial silence as Titivillus had done. Instead, as he cues on his first dupe, he allow us to accept his opening address as his own spoken thoughts bared in the safety of privacy: "Dive, thoughts, down to my soul—here Clarence comes!" He allows us, that is, to be eavesdroppers or onlookers who can share his wicked fun without acknowledging that we are implicated in it.[5]

Structurally, the next few sequences follow the pattern of the later moralities, where the dominant Vice ushered a series of victims on and off, working his wiles on each. Here, as there, our appreciation of the action depends primarily on the irony our awareness allows us to share with the manipulating knave as he plays his deceptive parts to one dupe after another. But Richard continues to play to our awareness without calling open attention to it, as the Vice had characteristically done through the self-explanatory asides that punctuated his dialogue. When Richard adopts that very technique later on and comments directly on its heritage ("Thus, like the formal Vice, Iniquity, / I moralize two meanings in one word"), the effect will be less winning than the one he manages here. In fact, it adds zest to the fun we have at Clarence's expense in the first sequence when Richard exchanges ironic winks and nods with *him* rather than with us, as though the two of them alone shared the mockery with which Richard turns Clarence's guard, Brakenbury, into a straight man:

> We speak no treason, man. We say the king
> Is wise and virtuous, and his noble queen
> Well struck in years, fair, and not jealous.
> We say that Shore's wife hath a pretty foot,
> A cherry lip, a bonny eye, a passing pleasing tongue;
> And that the queen's kindred are made gentlefolks.
> How say you, sir? Can you deny all this?
> (90–96)

Clarence had set himself up to be embraced by Richard's brotherly "we" when he started their interchange in a tone of familiar irony:

> *Rich*: Brother, good day. What means this armèd guard
>   That waits upon your grace?
> *Clar*:   His Majesty,

> Tend'ring my person's safety, hath appointed
> This conduct to convey me to the Tower.
> *Rich*: Upon what cause?
> *Clar*:   Because my name is George.
> (42–46)

Richard capitalizes on this opening masterfully, as he modulates from Clarence's own brave humor ("He should for that commit your godfathers"), to voicing Clarence's proper outrage and anxiety for him ("Why this it is, when men are ruled by women: / . . . We are not safe, Clarence—we are not safe"), to the consolations of brotherly love:

> Brother, farewell. I will unto the king;
> And whatsoe'er you will employ me in,
> Were it to call King Edward's widow sister,
> I will perform it to enfranchise you.
> Meantime, this deep disgrace in brotherhood
> Touches me deeper than you can imagine.
> (107–12)

We don't have to "imagine," of course. We know, and the comic pleasure of that knowledge, together with the superiority we share with Richard on the basis of it, is the primary response the dialogue has asked of us thus far. Since Richard doesn't ruffle the surface of that pleasure here by openly moralizing the two meanings we catch in one word (as in "I will deliver you, or else *lie* for you"), we need not be self-conscious about the sardonic humor we enjoy as he looks back at this first victim and then ahead to his next:

> Go, tread the path that thou shalt ne'er return:
> Simple plain Clarence, I do love thee so
> That I will shortly send thy soul to heaven.
> . . . . .
> . . . Then I'll marry Warwick's youngest daughter.
> What though I killed her husband and her father?
> The readiest way to make the wench amends
> Is to become her husband and her father.
> (117–19; 153–56)

The witty perversion of stolid proverbial wisdom to Richard's outrageous purposes ("But yet I run before my horse to market") becomes part of our sophisticated fun, and, as the first scene ends, we are given enough of Richard's "secret close intent" to prepare our enjoyment of the upcoming wooing scene from his ironic perspective. We are thus engaged into Richard's dramatic point of view without "identifying" ourselves with him. His grotesqueness, as my Introduction conjectures, may actually facilitate this sort of engagement by allaying whatever concern such an identification might cause us. In any case, his lack of other attractions for us, either physical or moral, indicates how exclusively the spirit we share with him here resides in the sport of his knavish art.

As though to heighten the odds against the astonishing peripety she undergoes in the second scene, Anne is given the stage to herself at its opening so that we can first see the depth of her bitter abhorrence of Richard without being distracted by his commanding presence. Until now his presentation and direction of all the action from the front of the stage had secured Richard's control over our point of view, but in this sequence and the next he enters a scene already set by his antagonists. Instead of thereby gaining the theatrical advantage over him, however, all the others manage to do in these instances is set the stage for him. The way they do so contradicts, in one sense, the image of them he had offered us in his opening speech. Rather than a world given over to the delightful measures of merry meetings from which Richard alone is excluded, we see the dead king's funeral, the dying king's court, and the grief and anxiety that darken both alike. We can scarcely expect Anne, as she escorts Lancastrian Henry's corpse, to be basking serenely in the Yorkist sun, of course. But it is really no brighter at court in the next scene, where Queen Elizabeth frets at a future shadowed by Richard Gloucester. If this general gloom belies Richard's sardonic sketch of "glorious summer," the effective contrast between his vitality and the dullness of the world at large, first established in that opening speech, is nonetheless enacted in the scenes that follow. He began by promising to explode the static lull of peace into action through his malcontent plots. In the second and third scenes, against these key-cold figures, these bloodless remnants, these pale ashes, Richard enters with all the theatrical momentum he had gathered in his first appearance. Since the active energy of the play is so exclusively his, we are naturally drawn to it. We will become more powerfully aware, as the play develops, of the deadly effect Richard's vitality has on all around him. Henry's cold corpse is only the first exhibit of that effect. But for now Richard's dramatic force carries us with him, as it carries Anne.

Anne's "obsequious lament" for dead Henry turns quickly into a series of curses aimed at the more lively center of our interest:

> O, cursèd be the hand that made these holes!
> Cursèd the heart that had the heart to do it!
> Cursèd the blood that let this blood from hence!
> (2.14–16)

In her series of curses, she plants the initial base of the ironic arch that will span her career in the play by wishing supreme misery on Richard's wife-to-be. By the time Anne rounds off that career by recalling her curse verbatim in act 4, we will have seen enough such neatly shaped and firmly emphasized retributions to be fully conscious that this repeated pattern of events is ultimately above Richard's control. Here, however, the primary effect of her curse, together with the repugnant images of spiders, toads, and creeping venomed things that Anne heaps on Richard, is to amplify our sense of his dynamic force by setting up the absolute odds against which he undertakes the very role he disclaimed with such apparent good reason in his opening speech: that of the lover. Our admiration for Richard's art must reach its peak at the end of this scene. We had smiled with him as he deluded "poor, simple Clarence," but to deceive a trusting brother was in itself no remarkable achievement. To woo the woman who loathes him at the very moment when her feelings against him are flowing full force—this, in the deformed crookback's own words, is "all the world to nothing." If it defies belief, he will express our own sense of wonder for us once he has brought it off. In the meantime, we can only watch in fascination as he skillfully transforms the railing widow into a coy mistress. Since we cannot have developed much emotional investment in Anne or her plight yet, the fact that we understand perfectly both the art and the irony of Richard's every move works to engage us with him throughout the sequence.

Richard enters with an aristocratic assumption of command that may remind us of his claim to be a soldier as well as a villain. He arrogantly reverses the charges that the conductors of this funeral have every right to lodge against his intrusion ("Unmannered dog! Stand thou when I command!") and quickly cows them into obedience. But their submissiveness is only the foil to Anne's bold, outspoken defiance. Her invective imputes any power this "lump of foul deformity" might have not to his knavish art but to his fiendish provenance ("mortal eyes cannot endure the devil"), and she holds her own against him for the nonce by simply converting his every verbal advance into its opposite and hurling it back at him:

> *Rich*: Sweet saint, for charity, be not so curst.
> *Anne*: Foul devil, for God's sake hence
> . . . . .
> *Rich*: Lady, you know no rules of charity.
> . . . . .
> *Anne*: Villain, thou know'st nor law of God nor man.
> . . . . .
> *Rich*: Vouchsafe, divine perfection of a woman,
>   Of these supposèd crimes to give me leave
>   By circumstance but to acquit myself.
> *Anne*: Vouchsafe, diffused infection of a man,
>   Of these known evils, but to give me leave
>   By circumstance t'accuse thy cursèd self.
> *Rich*: Fairer than tongue can name thee, let me have
>   Some patient leisure to excuse myself.
> *Anne*: Fouler than heart can think thee, thou canst make
>   No excuse current but to hang thyself.   (2.49–84)

The energy of her attack depends on her total commitment to the absolute terms of her opposition. She is right, of course, about those terms; as simple and stark as they are, they represent the truth about Richard in this play. If Richard's suit were no more subtle than this bland mixture of flattery and apology, Anne's hold on that truth would be firm enough to fend him off in this game of give and take, and thus far the match may seem an equal one. But that this is not Richard's game, that he has merely been allowing Anne to fix her stance so rigidly in order to knock her off balance, becomes apparent when he breaks through the increasingly predictable pattern of straight line and retort with a sudden, surprising, stichomythic thrust:

> *Anne*: He [Henry] is in heaven, where thou shalt never come.
> *Rich*: Let him thank me that holp to send him thither;
>   For he was fitter for that place than earth.
> *Anne*: And thou unfit for any place, but hell.
> *Rich*: Yes, one place else, if you will hear me name it.
> *Anne*: Some dungeon.
> *Rich*:   Your bedchamber.

While she gathers her breath, he adroitly shifts from what we now see to have been mere foreplay and begins his real assault:

> *Rich*:   But, gentle Lady Anne,
>   To leave this keen encounter of our wits
>   And fall something into a slower method—
>   Is not the causer of the timeless deaths
>   Of these Plantagenets, Henry and Edward,
>   As blameful as the executioner?
> *Anne*: Thou wast the cause and most accursed effect.
> *Rich*: Your beauty was the cause of that effect—
>   Your beauty, that did haunt me in my sleep
>   To undertake the death of all the world,
>   So I might live one hour in your sweet bosom.
> (2.106–24)

The pure logic of this "slower method" won't win her either, of course, and his open emergence as a lover provokes her most violent outbursts against him. But the turn here shows how artfully he is controlling their "keen encounter." He uses this next phase to prepare the way for his own "emotional" release, abandoning argument to show her the wonder that she alone can work—a Richard reduced, for the first time in his bitter life, to abject tears. Both his art and the irony on which it turns gain maximum intensity here. The irony is essentially the same that he had played on in a minor key in the first scene when he lamented, with Clarence, their powerlessness under the controlling sway of Edward's women. The manipulator claims to be manipulated throughout. But here he gives the screw an extra turn by openly admitting his crimes to Anne and then pinning sole responsibility for his slavish deeds on her commanding beauty. Then, having attributed absolute power to her, he makes her act out her true inability to do anything according to her own professed will by baring his breast to the sword he gives her. She cannot even command him to use the sword on himself. At the very moment she allows herself to believe she may be his prime mover, she shows her passivity, her malleability under his controlling hand, to be complete. As they subside from this emotional pitch into quiet concord, they resume the balanced pattern that had characterized their first set-to. There line had matched line to point up absolute opposition, but here each meets the other's rhythm in what feels more like the reciprocity of Romeo and Juliet's sonnet-dialogue at the Capulet's ball:

> *Anne*: I would I knew thy heart.
> *Rich*:   'Tis figured in my tongue.
> *Anne*: I fear me both are false.
> *Rich*:   Then never was man true.
> *Anne*: Well, well, put up your sword.
> *Rich*:   Say then my peace is made.
> *Anne*: That shalt thou know hereafter.
> *Rich*:   But shall I live in hope?
> *Anne*: All men, I hope, live so.
> *Rich*:   Vouchsafe to wear this ring.
> *Anne*: To take is not to give.[6]
> (2.192–202)

It is a marvelous tour de force, and at no point in the play do we share Richard's feelings more entirely than when (having ushered Anne out and disposed of the nearly forgotten corpse) he turns to exclaim with us: "Was ever woman in this humor wooed? / Was ever woman in this humor won?" (227–28). On this score we can be as awed by his accomplishment as he is pleased with himself; and the jaunty self-mockery with which he concludes this speech and the scene seals our mutual exhilaration:

> Shine out, fair sun, till I have bought a glass,
> That I may see my shadow as I pass.

This is, indeed, the dark villain's brightest moment, and our applause at his exit line must be wholeheartedly *for* him.

That the sun shines only for Richard, even among the Yorkists, is further brought home to us in the opening sequence of scene 3 as the tristful queen and her party face the dismal prospect of Edward's imminent death. Again, life is first breathed into this somber scene for us with Richard's entrance. Again, he is the active agent here, even though he enters a situation that is not (as the first two have been) entirely his own contrivance. And again we can savor the irony of his accusation that the Queen is the moving force behind the action of the play. We see her, poor helpless thing that she is, passively submissive to events beyond her control, unable even to summon up any positive wishful thinking:

> Would all were well! but that will never be:
> I fear our happiness is at the height.
> (3.40–41)

And in comes Richard, bursting upon the scene in feigned outrage at those who have abused him with "dissentious rumors." True, neither Elizabeth nor anyone else onstage is fooled in the least, so that our own awareness of Richard's playacting is not as elevated above them as it was over trusting Clarence and baffled Anne. As will happen at other points in the play, Richard's "guise" serves no actual deceptive purpose here and seems to be assumed primarily for the pleasure he takes in the bravado of it. And, as is characteristic of such knavish sport, his pleasure serves ours here as well. While the scene develops as a clash between Richard and the Queen's party, we enjoy it from his point of view, largely through the puckish irony of his assumed innocence:

> Cannot a plain man live and think no harm,
> But thus his simple truth must be abused
> With silken, sly, insinuating Jacks?
> (3.51–53)

But something happens here that suddenly expands and alters our perspective and thereby detaches our viewpoint from Richard's. With the entrance of the exiled Lancastrian dowager Margaret, who stands aside and comments on this intramural Yorkist squabble, we see Richard placed for the first time within a context beyond his control. He is subjected to a scrutiny of which he is unaware, and we share the intruding onlooker's consequent advantage over him. The result is that for the moment he shrinks to the level of an unconscious actor playing his part in a framework not of his making. Lines that we would otherwise simply enjoy with him for their shameless irony are glossed for us from another angle:

> *Rich*: Let me put in your minds, if you forget,
>   What you have been ere this, and what you are;
>   Withal, what I have been, and what I am.
> *Marg*: [aside] A murd'rous villain, and so still thou art.
>   . . . . .
> *Rich*: I am too childish-foolish for this world.
> *Marg*: [aside] Hie thee to hell for shame, and leave this world,
>   Thou cacodemon! there thy kingdom is.[7]
> (3.130–43)

Here Richard's pose is punctured (or at least punctuated) in a way he could not, in any case, control. But when Margaret steps forward and reveals herself, he loses control of his own ironic pose altogether. As he answers her charges in kind, he becomes for the moment merely one of the "wrangling pirates" onstage, responding instead of manipulating ("Foul wrinklèd witch, what mak'st thou in my sight?"), and thereby reducing himself in our eyes to the common plane of those with whom he interacts. The apparently unconscious irony in his righteous outburst seems indistinguishable from that which every susceptible wrongdoer in the play falls into when he leaves himself open to the very charge he hurls:

> His curses then, from bitterness of soul
> Denounced against thee, are all fall'n upon thee;
> And God, not we, hath plagued thy bloody deed.
> (3.178–80)

As Margaret points out, this curse can be answered in kind easily enough. She delivers the first of those several body counts in the play that sound like balanced credit sheets:

> Though not by war, by surfeit die your king,
> As ours by murder, to make him a king!
> Edward thy son, that now is Prince of Wales,
> For Edward our son, that was Prince of Wales,
> Die in his youth by like untimely violence!
> (3.196–200)

The depersonalization effected by the rigidly symmetrical rhetoric is perfectly apt. From the cosmic perspective of the retributive providential view that opens for us here, one king or one prince looks much like another, and debts are canceled with a life for a life. From this view, those who aspire to great things in the political world shrink to indistinguishable ciphers. It is a long view that the play allows us to share with those aged sufferers — Margaret here and the Duchess of York later — who are capable of it. Richard, whose keynote is "now" and who looks only to this world "to bustle in," is fundamentally incapable of it, which is why the larger irony of the play turns against him when he calls here all too righteously on the providential view of history to denounce Margaret.[8]

Once Margaret leaves, Richard quickly regains control of himself and of the more immediate irony he enjoys through his pious pose:

> I cannot blame her. By God's holy Mother,
> She hath had too much wrong, and I repent
> My part thereof that I have done to her.
> . . . . .
> I was too hot to do somebody good
> That is too cold in thinking of it now.
> (3.305–11)

But when Elizabeth and her party leave Richard alone, it is not only the absence of witty sparkle and the predominance of straight descriptive boasting that make the soliloquy in which he surveys himself and his accomplishments less winning for us than its counterpart at the end of the preceding scene had been:

> I do the wrong, and first begin to brawl.
> The secret mischiefs that I set abroach
> I lay unto the grievous charge of others.
> . . . . .
> And thus I clothe my naked villainy
> With odd old ends stol'n forth of holy writ,
> And seem a saint, when most I play the devil.
> (3.323–37)

The lines sum up (with uncharacteristic flatness) our ironic perspective as the play has developed it to the entrance of Margaret: Richard, the sole contriver of all actions, lays the charge of contrivance to his passive dupes. But Margaret has offered us a scopic view of things past and to come, within which Richard himself and all his contriving seem but a part of a larger scheme. Our dramatic sense would in any case validate the claim of this "lunatic" outsider, who steps into the play primarily in order to forecast the fate of each major character onstage, that she is a "prophetess." And of course our historical knowledge leaves no doubt that the dramatic pattern Margaret outlines when she predicts that Richard will ripen through others' miseries toward his own climactic downfall is in fact the one this play holds in store for us.[9] In the context Margaret has just alerted us to, then, Richard's smug boast of absolute control, unrelieved by any saving self-mockery, is overshadowed by an irony of which he is oblivious. The knavish *eiron* puffs himself up, through his vaunting soliloquy, into the vulnerable shape of an *alazon*.

The murder of Clarence in the scene that follows is again "directed" by Richard; but unlike any preceding scene, Richard does not appear in this one and does not therefore personally affect our responses to it. In his absence, attitudes that he has played to are reduced to a parody form through the agency of his lesser "mates," the two murderers. At the same time, the scene demands strong responses from us that work directly against the current of feeling that Richard controls. "Clarence," Richard had warned his hireling executioners, "is well-spoken, and perhaps / May move your hearts to pity if you mark him" (1.3.347–48). And before these two worthies get their chance to test their mettle against Clarence's appeals, we are made to mark him long and well. Clarence's imaginatively prophetic nightmare is, in a sense, as "plain and simple" as his trust in Richard. It presents no difficulty to our understanding; but the understanding to which it speaks is one that surpasses all sniggering delight in Richard's sportive tricks. The latter part of the dream — Clarence's imagined reception in hell — is akin to Margaret's curse (though more vivid) in its insistence on the punishment that inexorably awaits every crime. This firm pattern of retribution will, we must now sense, apply to Richard as well, and not least for the crime now under way. But the more telling subversion of Richard's aspiring contrivances comes in the first part of Clarence's dream. In the slow leisure of his painful nightmare-drowning, Clarence's eye is tortured with "sights of ugly death":

> Methoughts I saw a thousand fearful wracks;
> A thousand men that fishes gnawed upon;
> Wedges of gold, great anchors, heaps of pearl,
> Inestimable stones, unvaluèd jewels,
> All scatt'red in the bottom of the sea:
> Some lay in dead men's skulls, and in the holes
> Where eyes did once inhabit, there were crept
> (As 'twere in scorn of eyes) reflecting gems,
> That wooed the slimy bottom of the deep
> And mocked the dead bones that lay scatt'red by.
> (4.24–33)

We have seen Richard mock a corpse while he preens himself ("But first I'll turn yon fellow in his grave") and heard him commend eyes that "drop millstones when fools' eyes fall tears." But the gem in the eye of the skull gives back the ultimate mock, keener than the cold millstone. It is not just that this haunting image of mortality calls on our tear-falling pity for Clarence as he faces his own imminent death. The still, hard gem reflects back wryly on Richard's bustling activity in this "breathing world." All that energy will lead to this, for Richard's victims *and* for Richard himself. Clarence's dream-image of Richard tells both sides of that story:

> Methought that Gloucester stumblèd, and in falling
> Struck me (that thought to stay him) overboard
> Into the tumbling billows of the main.
> (4.18–20)

Here we see both the result of Richard's action and its final direction. The death maker, the "cockatrice . . . whose unavoided eye is murderous," is himself on his way down, not up, and his clever maneuvering is translated into a stumble, a fall toward "the slimy bottom of the deep" where that other witty wooer with jewels for eyes will mock his crooked bones.

Clarence's dream makes us feel the mortal anguish of a "Christian faithful man" stricken by the conscience of his own guilt in a world governed by a righteously vengeful God. The murder sequence that follows plays curiously to the various responses thus far evoked in us without letting any one of them predominate, though there is a movement here from blithe jocularity to dead seriousness that may reflect in little the movement of these first four scenes and of the play as a whole. We smile sardonically with (and at) Richard's tool villains as they dispatch troublesome conscience:

> I'll not meddle with it; it makes a man a coward. A man cannot steal, but it accuseth him; a man cannot swear, but it checks him; a man cannot lie with his neighbor's wife, but it detects him. 'Tis a blushing shame-faced spirit that mutinies in a man's bosom. It fills a man full of obstacles. . . . It is turned out of towns and cities for a dangerous thing, and every man that means to live well endeavors to trust to himself and live without it.
> (4.131–40)

We see the larger pattern of providential retribution, now at work on Clarence, that engulfs the smaller irony of Clarence's trust in Richard:

> Erroneous vassals! the great King of Kings
> Hath in the table of his law commanded
> That thou shalt do no murder.
> . . . . .
> Take heed; for he holds vengeance in his hand

To hurl upon their heads that break his law.
(4.190–95)

And we feel the pity and fear of Clarence's last moments as he pleads for his life. The murderers themselves cannot hold altogether firm against his appeals, and to some degree their rift at the end of the scene—the hard bravado of the First Murderer against the conscience-stricken vision of horror and sin in the Second Murderer—represents the opposite sides of our understanding that have been called on thus far in the play. But here bravado is stripped of Richard's engaging wit and exposed at its most "beastly, savage, [and] devilish" as the First Murderer stabs the pleading Clarence in the back. Abandoned by his repentant colleague, this stalwart is left alone onstage to close the sorry scene as best he can:

> Go, coward as thou art.
> Well, I'll go hide the body in some hole
> Till that the duke give order for his burial;
> And when I have my meed, I will away,
> For this will out, and then I must not stay.

Closure had been Richard's pleasure in each sequence until now; and the different spirit in which we responded to his similar directives ("Go, tread the path that thou shalt ne'er return: / Simple plain Clarence . . . ") and plans ("But first I'll turn yon fellow in his grave") measures the theatrical effect of his brash knavish humor on our point of view. None of the victims on which he worked directly in those sequences had been allowed to enlist our sympathy as Clarence has here, of course. But villainy is in any case easy to despise when it assumes a slinking posture ("And when I have my meed, I will away"). When it suits Shakespeare's purpose to disengage us further from Richard later on, one means of doing so will be to strip him of that "alacrity of spirit" that had made us enjoy so much of the play with him.

The third and fourth scenes, then, broaden our perspective and widen the range of our responses beyond the tight control Richard had exercised as contriver and presenter over our point of view at the beginning. But if we now see and feel more than

Richard himself can about his actions and his victims, it nonetheless remains true through much of what follows that whatever heightened awareness might detach us from Richard is not called into play very forcefully while he himself is onstage. Our revulsion against the murder of Clarence can be spent on the simple surrogate who executes it. In succeeding scenes, we alternate between choral accounts of Richard's "deep vice" and of the slaughterhouse that England has become under his deadly sway on the one hand and the lively, commanding presence of Richard himself on the other. As at the beginning, the fact that he alone makes anything happen naturally gives Richard a theatrical advantage. Edward's feeble and futile attempt at peacemaking in act 2, scene 1—the only tentative movement *not* directed by Richard through the first half of the play—simply sets off by contrast the ease with which Richard disrupts it when he enters to usurp the scene. This scene fits the pattern of several others (act 1, scene 2; act 1, scene 3; act 2, scene 2) through the first half of the play in which characters strike a solemn and static pose (grief; anxiety; hope) for Richard to play on as he will when he comes in. But what makes us appreciate these scenes from Richard's point of view more than the fact that he turns them in his direction is the knavish irony that he controls and that we alone share fully with him. Even on the few occasions when he falls unconsciously into the common larger ironic pattern of pronouncing his own ultimate sentence, as he does when he says of Clarence's death that "God will revenge it" (2.1.139), he does so with a cynical self-consciousness of the immediate irony (his pious attribution of his own crimes to others) that distinguishes his fateful forecast from those made by others. And most of the time Richard is in full control of the ironic game that provides our diversion through these scenes:

> I do not know that Englishman alive
> With whom my soul is any jot at odds
> More than the infant that is born to-night.
> I thank my God for my humility.
> (2.1.70–73)

The tragedy of Hastings, acted out at the very center of the play, nicely illustrates the disparity at this point between what we understand clearly enough during those still moments of reflection that punctuate the action and the way we are made to respond while the game is in progress. Hastings's quick reversal from secure mirth to wretched death provides a neat, small paradigm for the larger reversals of Buckingham and Richard that span it, arch within arch. In the larger view, all three are as one, as Hastings's exit line affirms: "They smile at me who shortly shall be dead" (3.4.107). In Hastings's retrospective recognition, we are offered this larger perspective with calm clarity; and Grey and Rivers, whose executions serve as a brief intermission betwen the two "acts" of Hastings's tragedy, remind us that Richard and Buckingham are waiting their turns on death row too:

> *Grey*: Now Margaret's curse is fall'n upon our heads,
>   When she exclaimed on Hastings, you, and I,
>   For standing by when Richard stabbed her son.
> *Riv*: Then cursed she Richard, then cursed she Buckingham,
>   Then cursed she Hastings. O, remember, God,
>   To hear her prayer for them, as now for us!
> (3.3.15–20)

We are bound to accept the validity of this larger pattern in which all three figures seem identical when it is stated thus. Yet as we watch Richard and Buckingham go to work on Hastings, we smile at him as their comic dupe rather than contemplating him as their exemplary model. It is the disparity between their craft and his folly, their directive control and his pliant gullibility that gives these sequences their dramatic force for us. Our amusement gains a sharper edge, surely, from Buckingham's own false security as he toys with Hastings:

> *Buck*: Who knows the Lord Protector's mind herein?
>   Who is most inward with the noble duke?
> .   .   .   .   .
>   Lord Hastings, you and he are near in love.
> *Hast*: I thank his grace, I know he loves me well.
> (3.4.7–14)

We savor the jest at a different level from the smirking Buckingham who thinks *himself* "most inward with the noble duke," since we have already smiled at him with Richard in precisely the same way that he smiles here at Hastings:

> My other self, my counsel's consistory,
> My oracle, my prophet, my dear cousin,
> I, as a child, will go by thy direction.
> (2.2.151–53)

But the concentric circles of this particular irony are contained by Richard. In the game of fool and knave, he is nobody's fool, and we enjoy that game with him whenever he plays it through the first three acts of the play.

The nature of the game changes somewhat as Richard gains effective political control of the realm through the Protectorship. In this position of power, his triumphs are less spectacularly "winning" for us than his early successes had been since they depend less on clever deception and more on the ruthless use of authority. Not that Richard is any less the counterfeiting knave through these scenes — it is here, in the middle of the play, that he coaches his apt accomplice Buckingham in the acting skills of "the deep tragedian" (3.5.1–11). But the parts are now played more to "grace" authority's "stratagems" (in Buckingham's terms) than to fool its victims. No one onstage believes Richard's outlandish charge that Hastings, as an accessory to "Edward's wife, that monstrous witch" and "that harlot, strumpet Shore" (a likely team!), is responsible for Richard's withered arm (3.4.59–78). This is what another abuser of authority would call "the *form* of justice," the merest show of legality with which raw power validates a political execution.[10] The choric citizens in act 2, scene 3 ("O, full of danger is the Duke of Gloucester"), and the moralizing Scrivener in act 3, scene 6, make it clear that such shows are seen plainly enough now by the world at large for what they are:

> Here's a good world the while! Who is so gross
> That cannot see this palpable device?
> Yet who's so bold but says he sees it not?

The Mayor who so obsequiously accepts the explanation of Hastings's sudden execution ("Your grace's words shall serve") may actually *be* gross enough not to see the palpable device; but more likely, he falls into the timorous category of those who see and dare not say they do.

Richard counts so heavily on such intimidation for the likes of the citizenry in general that he discards any gesture toward credibility as he prepares for the act that will crown his efforts. When he sends Buckingham to give a speech at the guildhall asserting Edward's bastardy and his own consequent legitimate claim to the throne—an argument that depends on such evidence as Richard's lineaments "being the right idea" of his father's, "both in . . . form and nobleness of mind"—he can only suppose that in such a setting his "grace's words shall serve," whatever the words may be. The failure of this palpable device is Richard's first frustration in the play:

> *Buck*: And when mine oratory drew to an end,
>   I bid them that did love their country's good
>   Cry, "God save Richard, England's royal king!"
> *Rich*: And did they so?
> *Buck*: No, so God help me, they spake not a word,
>   But, like dumb statues or breathing stones,
>   Stared each on other, and looked deadly pale.
> (3.7.20–26)

The terms are interesting, since they suggest that the cockatrice has the same effect in failure as in success: he can petrify, but not animate. But in the sweep of the action here, the frustration is negligible. Buckingham's planted stooges and the obliging Mayor will provide enough supporting voices for Richard to act out his reluctant acceptance of the burden of state from the beseeching multitudes.

This grand scene, then, is done for the form and the fun of it alone. No one need be fooled. And though we enjoy Richard's pious pose with the same ironic awareness that amused us in earlier scenes, the fact that no one is fooled gives us a somewhat different perspective. When we alone shared the joke with Richard at his dupe's expense, we were inevitably drawn into the scene from his point of view. When he acts in concert with others who know they are participating in a "palpable device," we can appreciate the nice touches in his treatment of "the maid's part," but we nonetheless take in the whole show from a more detached perspective. Our set here is much what it would be watching a televised interview of a "noncandidate" for the American presidency or a "spontaneous" demonstration at a nominating convention (the scene combines elements of both). Participants and audience alike accept denials and protestations on the one hand and the enthusiastic clamor on the other as the proper and expected form on such occasions. Richard handles the whole thing beautifully. But since everyone involved knows that the action here is stage-managed, we don't share his elevation over the others in the same way we did when he took in Clarence and Anne.

The scene in which Richard meets the two young princes and sends them to "repose" at the Tower (act 3, scene 1) is closer in kind to those earlier encounters and suggests even more clearly the different quality of Richard's success through the midpart of the play. Here, as there, Richard works his way on victims who have no awareness that they are being manipulated toward his ends. But the effect of his triumph on us is much less winning here. Though it might seem difficult to manage such a scene for our thorough enjoyment from Richard's point of view in any case, it is not simply our natural sympathy for these innocent boys that makes the difference. More telling is the extent to which they prove invulnerable to his guile and capable of actually stealing the show from him in a battle of wits, so that the very current that elsewhere draws us to Richard is turned against him. The scene exposes the fact that Richard has his way here through the force of his authority, not through the cunning of his knavery. It acts out, in effect, Elizabeth's image of Richard in the preceding scene:

> The tiger now hath seized the gentle hind;
> Insulting tyranny begins to jut
> Upon the innocent and aweless throne.
> (2.4.50–52)

Richard, of course, wraps his tiger's heart in a player's hide, and in a sense the boys are "fooled," since they don't suspect his ultimate aims against them and treat him on the whole as a good, gruff uncle. But Prince Edward turns aside his uncle's attempt to delude him about Rivers and Grey with a clear-eyed rightness that belies Richard's patronizing speech on innocent youth's inability to distinguish true from false: "God keep me from false friends!—but they were none" (3.1.16). What we see as the scene progresses is not Richard manipulating the Prince verbally, but Richard muttering ominous asides our way as a foreboding commentary on the Prince's aspirations toward good kingship: "So wise so young, they say, do never live long" (79). Rather than directing what the Prince thinks and says, the best Richard can do here is to hide his own line of thought from the Prince behind a double meaning "like the formal Vice, Iniquity" (82). And when the younger brother, York, enters and engages Richard in a verbal wit-match, it is the boy who wins the appreciation of the onstage audience, as he must win ours:

> With what a sharp-provided wit he reasons!
> To mitigate the scorn he gives his uncle,
> He prettily and aptly taunts himself:
> So cunning, and so young, is wonderful.
> (132–135)

Richard needn't be wonderfully cunning with the young princes, of course. As Lord Protector, he can lodge them in the Tower on the simple grounds that he "needs will have it so" (141). But using his authority to imprison two boys already wise enough to turn aside his "palpable device" and sharp enough to win a round from him in the game of wits gains a far different response from us than his audacious wooing of Anne, where the odds against his knavery were "all the world to nothing."

If we have different feelings toward Richard through the scene with the princes than we had earlier, it is not because what he does is more reprehensible, but because the way he does it is less engaging. Child-murder may be even more repugnant than fratricide, but our responses don't depend on such calculations. They depend rather on the way the scenes are played to us.[11] Richard has been vicious enough to outrage any moral sensibility from the very beginning, but as long as we are made to enjoy the action with the flow of Richard's own enjoyment, outrage won't be our primary response to him. And in spite of his less winning performance with the princes, his fun and ours are nearly

identical through the first three acts of the play. More and more
we are given the larger moral and providential perspective within
which we are asked to see, place, and judge the murderous
cockatrice; but as long as this perspective is offered in those
intervals between his own lively appearances, whatever assent it
gains from us remains discrete from our primary theatrical
experience of him. When the foreseen providential judgment
against Richard finds its dramatic agent in Richmond, our way
of responding to Richard in action will have to change if our
official approval of his defeat is to carry any theatrical force. In
fact, the play works in several ways to make us welcome the
resolution that Richmond provides as we could not if we
continued to enjoy and anticipate Richard's sport with him.

Chaucer's Monk would mark the turn in Richard's tragedy in
act 4, scene 2, where we first see him in his coveted crown: having
reached this "greet prosperitee," the simple law of medieval tragic
gravity dictates that he will now fall "out of heigh degree / Into
myserie, and [end] wrecchedly." Several clear signs within the
play point out the direction the action must now take. The name
of Richmond, first mentioned in the previous scene as a
counterforce around which his hitherto helpless foes can rally,
begins to ring insistently within Richard's hollow crown. And as
he prepares to meet this ominous challenge, Margaret, who
foretold his fall along with those of the other Yorkists, enters
once more to announce that the time is ripe:

> So now prosperity begins to mellow
> And drop into the rotten mouth of death.
> . . . . .
> A dire induction am I witness to,
> And will to France, hoping the consequence
> Will prove as bitter, black, and tragical.
> (4.4.1–7)

The "inductions dangerous" of which Richard spoke in his
opening speech are now completed, and we await expectantly,
along with Margaret, the inevitable consequence.

As the narrative signals its major turn through these sequences,
a corresponding change takes place in the way we are made to
look at Richard. "None are for me," he now observes, "that look

into me with considerate eyes" (4.2.29–30). Given what he is, that is bound to be true, and the more we are made to look into him and consider him rather than smiling with him, the more our theatrical response adjusts itself to what any "considerate" view must be. His first appearance as King also offers us the first extended view of him that involves neither the manipulative role-playing nor the stylized self-portraits that he has undertaken for his amusement and ours throughout the play. "Stand all apart" is Richard's inauspicious keynote as King, and as the scene develops, he detaches himself not only from his court in general and his would-be colleague Buckingham in particular, but from us as well.[12] Isolation is not new for Richard in the play; we have known him to be "himself alone" from the beginning. But he has never before left *us* apart as he does here. Though we hear him plan his next moves as before, he neither plays to us in soliloquies and asides nor plays to others for our informed entertainment. Instead we become an audience along with the court as they watch him vent his frustration at Buckingham's sudden attack of cold feet: "The king is angry. See, he gnaws his lip." *That* is no act, and for once even the onstage observers are allowed to scrutinize an unmasked Richard. More privileged than they, we can hear the thoughts that begin to gnaw Richard internally as well:

> I do remember me Henry the Sixth
> Did prophesy that Richmond should be king
> When Richmond was a little peevish boy.
> A king!—perhaps—perhaps—
> (94–97)

Unlike those soliloquies through which Richard posed himself for our appreciation, this sort of "internal" monologue is designed precisely to let us look into the man in an unguarded moment, and to look "with considerate eyes." The thoughts in which he loses himself suggest plainly enough that he is also losing control of events:

> I must be married to my brother's daughter,
> Or else my kingdom stands on brittle glass:
> Murder her brothers, and then marry her—

This last reflection would have been the making of a sardonic joke for the earlier Richard, but now it prompts unwonted qualms:

> Uncertain way of gain! But I am in
> So far in blood that sin will pluck on sin.
> (59–63)

If we had been made to share anxieties from the beginning with Richard (as with Macbeth), it would be possible to feel with (or at least for) his sense of his predicament. But Richard's only hold on our point of view has been through the sort of callous wit that makes light of such human fears, and he loses that hold here as he loses the self-assured control that is essential to his knavish sport. We watch and consider while he chafes and worries.

If he begins to fret, Richard does not merely fret the time away. While Buckingham catches his breath offstage, Richard plans the murder of the princes. And in the next scene, when Tyrrel brings him the "happy news" that the boys are in fact dead, he regains his sportive good humor as he sums up what's been done and looks ahead:

> The son of Clarence have I pent up close,
> His daughter meanly have I matched in marriage,
> The sons of Edward sleep in Abraham's bosom,
> And Anne my wife hath bid this world good night.
> Now, for I know the Britain Richmond aims
> At young Elizabeth, my brother's daughter,
> And by that knot looks proudly on the crown,
> To her go I, a jolly thriving wooer.
> (4.3.36–43)

But if this sounds like the old Richard, his mood is not allowed to control the scene or our responses to it as it once had. Such buoyant soliloquies had capped the first and second scenes of the play, where Richard had virtually cued the entrances and exits of others whose interactions with him we then watched from his controlling perspective. But here Richard's speech is itself framed in a context that gives us perspective on his triumphant mood. Tyrrel opens the scene with an elaborate appeal to our revulsion against "the tyrannous and bloody act . . ., / The most arch

deed of piteous massacre / That ever yet this land was guilty of."
Unlike Anne's earlier lament over the "pale ashes" of key-cold
Henry, Tyrrel's description of the fresh, growing lives that have
been rooted out makes it clear that vitality was the victim here:

> Their lips were four red roses on a stalk,
> Which in their summer beauty kissed each other.
> . . . . .
>   We smotherèd
> The most replenishèd sweet work of nature
> That from the prime creation e'er she framèd.
> (12–19)

When he then cues on "the bloody king," the ironic ring of his
greeting ("All health, my sovereign lord!") tells in this context
directly against the "lump of foul deformity" who enters. Given
such an opening, we can scarcely share Richard's exuberance.
Nor is he allowed to close the scene with his "thriving" plans.
Ratcliffe bursts in upon him with the news that Richmond, the
bugaboo of Henry's prophecy, is gathering force like a thunder-
head. Richard responds vigorously enough, but it is symptomatic
of his diminishing control that he must now spend himself in
defensive countermoves as the energy of initiative in the play
shifts away from him to Richmond.

The first countermove is the suit to Elizabeth for her
daughter's hand (act 4, scene 4), undertaken not in the aspiring
mood in which Richard had assailed Anne, but as a defensive
measure because "the Britain Richmond aims / At young
Elizabeth." If the earlier suit had shown us Richard's most
winning performance, the parallel scene with Elizabeth gives us
a very different feeling. Richard's methodical, callous arguments
are now unrelieved by any spirit of bold fun or gamesmanship. In
spite of his own advance billing, he proves neither jolly nor
thriving as a wooer here.

Similarities in the structure of the two wooing scenes only
underline the differences in effect. Here as before, Richard enters
to find the object of his suit already pouring out her well-founded
hatred of him. But whereas Henry's funeral procession and
Anne's lament served primarily as a foil to the surging energy
with which Richard turned that situation around, the long

opening sequence here in which the stricken Yorkist women join their former antagonist Margaret in both dirge and curse carries a somber weight that seems to stifle Richard's attempts to disperse it when he finally comes on with his royal train. Margaret provides the keynote with her description of Yorkist prosperity now turned mellow and dropping into death's rotten mouth. As the women tally up their losses, they focus on Richard as the uncommon cause of their common grief:

> From forth the kennel of thy womb hath crept
> A hellhound that doth hunt us all to death:
> That dog, that had his teeth before his eyes,
> To worry lambs and lap their gentle blood,
> That foul defacer of God's handiwork,
> That excellent grand tyrant of the earth
> That reigns in gallèd eyes of weeping souls,
> Thy womb let loose to chase us to our graves.
> (47–54)

There is nothing new about such vituperation in itself, though it may now gain force from the treatment of the murdered princes in the preceding scene. And now, as well, every image that builds Richard up as the foul monster whose wake is strewn with the play's several corpses adds weight to Margaret's announcement (has she ever been wrong?) that his hour has come round at last:

> Richard yet lives, hell's black intelligencer;
> ·   ·   ·   ·   ·
>   But at hand, at hand,
> Ensues his piteous and unpitied end.
> Earth gapes, hell burns, fiends roar, saints pray,
> To have him suddenly conveyed from hence.
> (71–76)

It had been Richard's way to enter a scene set by others and steal it from them with gleeful ease. But in the face of the "copious . . . exclaims" that the wretched queens have piled up against him here, he makes decidedly his feeblest showing to date. Again the parallel with the earlier wooing scene is instructive. There, coming on alone to interrupt the funeral procession, he had usurped command at once: "Stay, you that bear the corse, and set it down." Here, entering with his own pompous procession, he is stymied by the women who stand in his way: "Who intercepts me in my expedition?" (136). In a petty use of the trappings of power, he resorts to a flourish of trumpets and drums rather than any exercise of wit to counter their "telltale" questions about his long line of victims. It is as though he has gone more stale than mellow in his "prosperity." There is little amusing in his testy responses to his mother's charges against him—his one attempt at a joke about Humphrey Hour is surely the flattest in the play. And after the Duchess offers a final maternal malediction and exits, his protracted proposition to Elizabeth falls just as flat. It is perfectly static, lacking any of the development, tension, or irony that Richard had controlled so adroitly in his encounter with Anne. Every bald appeal to self-interest, every palpable device, is met firmly with the retorts that Elizabeth has so plentifully at her disposal. What little spirit of irony emerges here springs out of her sarcastic anger, and Richard is reduced to the role of straight man, serving up line after line that will be turned back on him: "You mock me, madam; this is not the way / To win your daughter" (284–85). After 200 stalemated lines, it can only come as a total surprise to us when Elizabeth apparently succumbs to the mixture of pleading promises and bullying threats that Richard musters up as a coup de grace.

It is a perplexing moment in the play. We learn in the next scene that Elizabeth in fact gives her daughter to Richmond instead. But if we were to enjoy the full ironic effect of Richard as the smug duper duped in his exchange with Elizabeth, we would need some more open pointers than the dialogue gives us.[13] Nonetheless, whether or not we are made to see Richard as the foolish loser of this match, nothing leads us to admire him as the crafty winner. Whereas he had savored with us our wonder at his conquest of Anne in a tone of jovial self-mockery, here he barely has time to spit out his perhaps unwarranted scorn for Elizabeth ("Relenting fool, and shallow, changing woman") before he is deluged by the news of Richmond's advances. As the messengers pour in, what we see, in stark contrast to the early Richard who made life his own play for our entertainment by so masterfully directing the course of action, is a Richard who loses control of himself under the sudden rush of events: giving hasty orders and then fitfully canceling them, sending messengers off but forgetting to send the message, striking out at a third messenger before he even hears his news (which happens, for a change, to be good). He still has all the energy of the activist, but it now betrays itself as nervous energy, and the activity has the air of frenzy. To "considerate eyes" it looks not at all like the knavish sport with which he engaged us in his early schemes.[14]

From this point on, as the action moves to Bosworth field for the final confrontation, the play turns into a series of juxta-positions that work to Richard's disadvantage, preparing us to applaud the downfall of the villain whose earlier triumphs had entertained us. The absolute contrast between Richard and Richmond is developed through systematically paralleled se-quences in which the opposing leaders ready themselves and their troops for the showdown and, most memorably, receive their battle-eve charges from the dream-ghosts of Richard's many victims. Richmond is all that he must be to make the contrast between princely virtue and tyrannical vice complete — and that is *all* he is. No characterizing touch is allowed to complicate the single and pure function he is to serve. From his first lines to his last he soothes us with simple piety and with allegiance to the ideals of healthy fruition, peaceful union, and comradeship that set off Richard's sterile solitude and deadly blight:

> Fellows in arms, and my most loving friends,
> . . . . .
> In God's name cheerly on, courageous friends,
> To reap the harvest of perpetual peace.
> (5.2.1–15)

> And then, as we have ta'en the sacrament,
> We will unite the White Rose and the Red.
> Smile heaven upon this fair conjunction.
> . . . . .
> O, now let Richmond and Elizabeth,
> The true succeeders of each royal house,
> By God's fair ordinance conjoin together!
> And let their heirs (God, if thy will be so)

> Enrich the time to come with smooth-faced peace,
> With smiling plenty, and fair prosperous days!
> (5.5.18–34)

Sounding this one note, Richmond could not have interested us much if he had had to vie with Richard as a dramatic attraction from the beginning. But Shakespeare holds him off until the conclusion, where he need not provoke our interest. Richard has done that, and when our involvement with him has run its course from the initial engagement to the now expected downfall, all Richmond need do is provide a secure resting place for the resolution.

But until that resolution our interest remains focused much more intensely on Richard's villainy than on Richmond's virtue. The trick here is for Richard to keep his hold on our interest without holding our point of view in line with his as he had earlier on. One means of changing our point of view in the final scenes is to invert the way we are made to see the disparity between the "true" Richard and his public show. Earlier, we had enjoyed the irony of Richard's "act" with him on the basis of the prior and superior knowledge we shared through his private revelations to us. But now the whole presentation of Richard "acting" and Richard "behind the scenes" changes. At Bosworth, we see him in his public role as the bluff military commander—a sort of Faulconbridge or Hotspur—and we have no reason thus far to doubt the courageous notes with which he rallies his followers:

> Norfolk, we must have knocks. Ha! must we not?
> . . . . .
> Up with the tent! Come, noble gentlemen,
> Let us survey the vantage of the ground.
> Call for some men of sound direction:
> Let's lack no discipline, make no delay,
> For, lords, to-morrow is a busy day.
> (5.3.5–18)

Occasionally his Hotspur betrays a Falstaffian twinge within ("Here will I lie to-night; / But where to-morrow? Well, all's one for that"), but on the whole he keeps the part up firmly enough, both in this sequence and on the day of the battle itself.

Contained between these exhibitions of public bravado, therefore, the private night scene in the tent has all the quality of exposure. Here, revealed to our considerate eyes, is the cringing inner man beneath the hearty soldier's mask.

The Richard we see here is stripped of every quality that made his knavery winning in the opening scenes. He sums up the essential difference himself:

> I have not that alacrity of spirit
> Nor cheer of mind that I was wont to have.
> (5.3.73–74)

The fun has gone with the buoyant self-confidence that supported it. The man who earlier sized up the situation and then manipulated it to his own ends now frets anxiously at the clock he cannot control as his doomsday hour draws near. When he wakes out of the nightmare in which the long line of his victims' ghosts merges at the end into a prophetic vision of his final moments of defeat in battle ("Give me another horse! Bind up my wounds!"), we get a last soliloquy from him that is in every way the opposite of his first. There, in the neatly balanced syntax of his sure control, he had directed our view of the general scene and of his own place in it. Now his soliloquy springs out of the depths of a dream-consciousness he cannot control. And as he tries futilely to regain control through the fits and starts of a colloquy with his now divided self, he is exposed to us willy-nilly rather than displaying himself to us at his pleasure:

> O coward conscience, how dost thou afflict me!
> The lights burn blue. It is now dead midnight.
> Cold fearful drops stand on my trembling flesh.
> What do I fear? Myself? There's none else by.
> Richard loves Richard: that is, I am I.
> Is there a murderer here? No. Yes, I am:
> Then fly. What, from myself? Great reason why—
> Lest I revenge. What, myself upon myself?
> Alack, I love myself. Wherefore? For any good
> That I myself have done unto myself?
> O no! Alas, I rather hate myself
> For hateful deeds committed by myself.

I am a villain. Yet I lie, I am not.
Fool, of thyself speak well. Fool, do not flatter.
My conscience hath a thousand several tongues,
And every tongue brings in a several tale,
And every tale condemns me for a villain.
(180–96)

Only the name he chooses for himself remains the same: villain.
All the difference between his first speech and this one is summed
up in the *feel* of that word for him and (through him) for us, from
the swaggering audacity of his determination "to prove a villain"
to the cowering disgust that would disown the label if he could.
Whatever spark of telltale conscience flickers in the self-
condemnation has no positive moral force. It is truly enough a
"coward conscience," the fear of "tomorrow's vengeance on the
head of Richard." When he whimpers of this fear to Ratcliffe and
contrives his last "scheme," he reaches his lowest ebb:

'Tis not yet near day. Come, go with me.
Under our tents I'll play the easedropper,
To see if any mean to shrink from me.
(221–23)

The former sole master of events now is utterly dependent on
what he should know to be the nonexistent supportive bond of
his "friends": "Will our friends prove all true?" (214). And off he
goes to squat in the dark and eavesdrop helplessly on *their* plans,
shrinking as he goes to the very image of his enemies' curses: the
night-crawler with cold fearful drops on his trembling flesh, the
"bottled spider" and "foul bunch-backed toad".

We are now set for the kill, as totally primed for the conclusion
as we were eager for "inductions" when Richard opened the play.
That conclusion can only go one way, nor would we have it any
other: "There is no creature loves me; / And if I die, no soul will
pity me" (201–2). Love and pity, of which Richard had so long
both boasted and proved himself incapable, are not, as he points
out, responses he can now expect of us. And the sportive humor
that had been the single but powerful current uniting our
appreciation with his wit is lost. We now want what he dreads—
the end.

If that end holds any surprise for us at all, it is in the bravado that Richard manages to muster after the dark night of his terrified soul. Having reduced him to a whimper, Shakespeare allows his villain to go out with a bang—a finale more to our theatrical liking than the cringing wretch of the night scene could have provided. And the focus of the battle scenes is still on Richard, who continues to hold our central interest to the end. But if his battlefield panache impresses us once more, the basis of it is virtually the opposite of the bold wit that had engaged us early on. There his command of the true state of things gave him an advantage he shared only with us over those dupes who knew not his heart. Here his audacity is in pure defiance of the true state of things. In keeping with his credo of being "himself alone," he does not conclude the common pattern of providential retribution in the common way. All who had fallen before him articulated their tragedies in a final moment of clear-sighted retrospection. Buckingham, the last to do so, typifies the others in his recognition of a clear moral order in his experience:

> This is the day which in King Edward's time
> I wished might fall on me when I was found
> False to his children and his wife's allies;
> This is the day wherein I wished to fall
> By the false faith of him whom most I trusted;
> This, this All Souls' day to my fearful soul
> Is the determined respite of my wrongs:
> That high All-seer which I dallied with
> Hath turned my feignèd prayer on my head
> And given in earnest what I begged in jest.
> Thus doth He force the swords of wicked men
> To turn their own points in their masters' bosoms;
> Thus Margaret's curse falls heavy on my neck:
> "When he," quoth she, "shall split thy heart with sorrow,
> Remember Margaret was a prophetess."—
> Come lead me, officers, to the block of shame.
> Wrong hath but wrong, and blame the due of blame.
> (5.1.13–29)

An ironist himself in his heyday, Buckingham now sees his career by the light of the larger providential irony that has flashed over the play for us from the third scene on. The ironist Richard has also set himself up as a dupe for the larger irony of Providence (as in "God will revenge it" [2.1.139]) — the last, best dupe of all. And in the throes of his nightmarish fright on Bosworth eve, Richard too looks back along the arch of his tragic career and seems ready to interpret it in the common terms of sin and retribution that the others adopt in their final moments:

> My conscience hath a thousand several tongues,
> And every tongue brings in a several tale,
> And every tale condemns me for a villain.
> Perjury, perjury, in the highest degree,
> Murder, stern murder, in the direst degree,
> All several sins, all used in each degree,
> Throng to the bar, crying all, "Guilty! guilty!"
> (5.3.194–200)

But this is not Richard's final moment. And when he resumes the role of intrepid soldier on the morrow, we must marvel at the audacity with which he denies a truth writ so large in every sign around him. Therefore, though our focus of interest is on him through the battle, our awareness is at odds with his every attempt to rally himself:

> The sun will not be seen to-day;
> The sky doth frown and low'r upon our army.
> I would these dewy tears were from the ground.
> Not shine to-day? Why, what is that to me
> More than to Richmond? For the selfsame heaven
> That frowns on me looks sadly upon him.
> (5.3.283–88)

> Slave, I have set my life upon a cast,
> And I will stand the hazard of the die.
> (5.4.9–10)

The ironist disappears altogether in these heroic but foolhardy lines. There is no hazard in this cast. We know just how the providential dice are loaded, and insofar as Richard convinces himself to the contrary, he forsakes the primary hold that he (as a clear-sighted knavish manipulator) has had on our point of view. We see him literally lose himself in his final role.[15]

Richmond's grand peroration is designed to send us home thoroughly content that the horrors we have witnessed are washed away with the crippled corpse of their sole perpetrator. "The bloody dog is dead," and all's well. None of Shakespeare's other histories leaves us with such a gratifying sense of closure at the end. *Richard III* is easy on us in this respect, as it is in its use of the knavish villain who has been its vital attraction. The dynamics of our theatrical relationship with Richard are masterfully controlled in a way that forces no second thoughts or sudden questions upon us. If we enjoyed Richard on his own knavish terms at the beginning, we are nonetheless finally allowed to rest in peace. Marlowe, more a gadfly than the Shakespeare who wrote this play, will scarcely be so generous when he confronts us with his almost indestructible Jewish knave.

2

Barabas

STAGECRAFT VS. STATECRAFT

Knaves naturally dominate the actions they direct through their schemes. Few, however, steal quite so much of the show as Barabas, who leaves a meager half of the dialogue for the other twenty characters in *The Jew of Malta* to divide among themselves.[1] When he chooses the emblem for his own knavery, it is the serpent rather than the fox: "Now will I show myself to have more of the serpent than the dove; that is, more knave than fool" (2.3.36–37). And true to the adage, the snake has all the lines. In keeping with his knave's role, much of what Barabas says is for our ears only, either by way of soliloquy or aside. Yet, for all this prominent exposure, we have trouble getting a hold on the Jew, who proves to be a slippery serpent indeed — not so much because he is more complex than other knaves, but because he is more evasive. Evasiveness violates the normal rules of our relationship with knaves, who fool everyone else but are "honest" with us. Barabas fools us on occasion as well, which is one reason why our relationship with this buoyant knave is such a volatile one. If our interactions with Richard followed a reasonably neat curve to a comfortable conclusion, the strategy of Marlowe's play is altogether different. He clearly shares some of the sentiment his horrific Jew hurls from the cauldron at those who watch him boil: "I would have brought confusion on you all" (5.5.84). The play repeatedly knocks our conventionally self-flattering expectations off-balance through the responses to Barabas it demands from us. Although Marlowe uses the morality play's tactics of alienating us from the malicious knave who entertains us, he puts his own special twist on them; for much of what is "worst" in us, in conventional moral terms, is brought out through our rejection (as well as our appreciation) of the Jew.[2]

The Jew of Malta opens with the first of its surprising resurrections:

> Albeit the world think Machiavel is dead,
> Yet was his soul but flown beyond the Alps,
> And, now the Guise is dead, is come from France,
> To view this land, and frolic with his friends.

Part of the surprise here, for the first audience, would have been the very confrontation with the sardonic, impious Prologue who presents this play. The normal behavior for Prologues was courteous address, and their normal function straight, informative explication of the piece to follow.[3] But Machiavel approaches us here more in the manner of the Vice, Nichol Newfangle, than in that of the solemn Prologue who put the audience of *Like Will to Like* in the "right" frame of mind before Nichol ever got a shot at them. Of course Machiavel's assault, like Nichol's, is designed to provoke a nonresponse; none of us will wave back when he greets his English "friends," and to that extent we disclaim any association with him. The "lecture" he reads us "here in Britain," however, speaks directly to such disclaimers in a way that makes the moralist's position in the audience a difficult one to maintain comfortably.

We can suppose a pause after the initial greeting, allowing us to reject, for *our* part, the imputed friendship.[4] But then Machiavel takes us up on just this point:

> To some, perhaps, my name is odious,
> But such as love me, guard me from their tongues, . . .

The syntax is ambiguous thus far, and offers a suggestion of what will be spelled out in a moment: the true admirers of Machiavel never praise him—what we are and what we say are two different things.[5] First, however, the ambiguity is resolved into another meaning:

> And let them know that I am Machiavel,
> And weigh not men, and therefore not men's words.

He is, apparently, ordering his friends to guard him from the
verbal attacks of his enemies. But he goes on immediately to
expose those "enemies" for what they really are:

> Admir'd I am of those that hate me most:
> Though some speak openly against my books,
> Yet will they read me, and thereby attain
> To Peter's chair; and when they cast me off,
> Are poison'd by my climbing followers.

This division of the world into two kinds of Machiavels, the open
advocates (but where are *they* among us?) and the secret
admirers, puts a snaffle in disapproval's mouth. Our very
rejection of the creed that follows identifies us, in such a world,
as covert Machiavels.

As it turns out, the brief lecture in the fundamentals of his
creed that Machiavel now offers would work as a prologuelike
explication of the play to be presented, though not a morally
palatable one:

> I count religion but a childish toy,
> And hold there is no sin but ignorance.
> . . . . .
> Hence comes it, that a strong-built citadel
> Commands much more than letters can import.
> Which maxim had Phalaris observ'd
> H' had never bellowed in a brazen bull.

So, it must appear at the end of the play, if Barabas had actually
observed his master's maxims, he never would have bellowed in a
boiling cauldron. And insofar as the play prompts us toward this
astute observation on Barabas's final "sin of ignorance," it proves
upon us the very claim Machiavel has just made about those of
us who profess him not: we know how the world really works
nonetheless and can judge Barabas's fall accordingly. In fact, the
play shows us a world divided just along the lines the Prologue
has drawn for ours. On the one hand, there is Barabas, whose
stage villainy makes him all too apparent a Machiavel; on the

other, Ferneze, on whose cold lips the master's name would never appear and who is therefore a more truly effective disciple.

But we cannot anticipate such application without more direct help from the Prologue; and, instead of offering that, Machiavel passes his instruction off as the characteristic digression of an enthusiastic teacher:

> But whither am I bound? I come not, I,
> To read a lecture here in Britain,
> But to present the tragedy of a Jew,
> Who smiles to see how full his bags are cramm'd,
> Which money was not got without my means.
> I crave but this: grace him as he deserves,
> And let him not be entertain'd the worse
> Because he favors me.

If being buttonholed by this disconcerting cynic has made us squirm somewhat, we can relax when he turns to the proper business of our afternoon's entertainment and presents it in the form of such a blatant caricature. Machiavel, who should have been an easy target for our hisses, posed some problems that we might prefer not to consider. But a greedy Jew fondling his ill-gotten gains? We know well enough how to "grace *him* as he deserves"![6]

Barabas's appearance in his countinghouse, red-wigged and bottle-nosed, seems to confirm the stereotype Machiavel had promised us. The Jew's first speech, however, quickly bursts the ordinary limits of such an easily placed (and easily despised) image. He dazzles us, not only with the extent of his wealth ("infinite riches in a little room"), but with his grand disdain for paltry silver ("Fie! what a trouble 'tis to count this trash"), with the Tamburlainian scope that distinguishes his "means of traffic from the vulgar trade," and perhaps most of all through his apparent alliance with the natural forces that send the riches of the world his way:

> But now how stands the wind?
> Into what corner peers my halcyon's bill?
> Ha! to the east? yes: see how stands the vanes?
> East and by south. Why then I hope my ships

> I sent for Egypt and the bordering isles
> Are gotten up by Nilus' winding banks:
> Mine argosy from Alexandria,
> Loaden with spice and silks, now under sail,
> Are smoothly gliding down by Candy shore
> To Malta, through our [!] Mediterranean sea.
> (38–47)

Like a Prospero on a grander scale, Barabas almost seems able to exert his will over wind and sea. What we took at first to be a miserly countinghouse seems transformed into a magician's control tower. But by what special dispensation could Barabas be granted these powers? By all rights, such arrogance in a heathen Jew should be dashed, and yet the succeeding sequence justifies it utterly. A merchant rushes in hailing the safe return of Barabas's ships "richly fraught": "The very custom barely comes to more / Than many merchants of the town are worth." Barabas need not stir from his "little room" to conduct his business at the custom house, where his "title" alone stands credit for such a sum:

> Go tell 'em the Jew of Malta sent thee, man:
> Tush, who amongst 'em knows not Barabas?
> (66–67)

There are other Jews in Malta, as we shall see; but everyone knows who *the* Jew of Malta is. And not only can he use that title as a password to open customhouse doors; he can defy the laws of chance at will. His seamen wonder at his apparent recklessness with his Alexandrian argosy, wonder how he "durst with so much wealth / Trust such a crazed vessel, and so far." But Barabas brushes aside their paltry worries (what do mere sailors know about ships?): "Tush; they are wise! I know her and her strength" (77–80). And once again his arrogant assurance is rewarded by a second breathless merchant, who appears as though conjured by Barabas's very mention of this ship, which now rides safe "in Malta road, / Laden with riches, and exceeding store / Of Persian silks, of gold, and orient pearl" (84–87). Taking this news in stride, Barabas quickly surveys all naval activity on the Mediterranean with a few adroit questions and sure surmises.

Incredible! There he sits in his command post, making the world turn around him, summoning all its wealth to him—and with such evident ease!

The point I would emphasize first about this exhibition of the Jew's power is that there is, as yet, virtually nothing knavish about it. Barabas sees all and controls all, but not by means of the engaging schemer's witty intrigue, and therefore there are no ironic overtones for us to savor with him and no manipulation of other characters through a plot he shares with us for our mutual entertainment. He simply *displays* his power and his glory to us. Such power commands our wonder. In the hands of a beneficent Prospero it might also command our respect. But that this *Jew* should wield it exclusively for his own extravagant enrichment—this can only provoke the envy that his master Machiavel had identified as the natural response of "poor, petty wights" to those who hold power. Everything in the first hundred lines has been designed to encourage such a response; and, having dismissed his second messenger of good fortune, Barabas turns to us once more and rubs our seemly anti-Semitic noses in our own envy:

> Thus trolls our fortune in by land and sea,
> And thus are we on every side enrich'd:
> These are the blessings promis'd to the Jews,
> And herein was old Abram's happiness.
> What more may heaven do for earthly man
> Than thus to pour out plenty in their laps,
> Ripping the bowels of the earth for them,
> Making the sea their servants, and the winds
> To drive their substance with successful blasts?
> (101–9)

That is just what has already been sticking in our Christian throats. Heaven is raining its plenty on this Jew, pouring it into his lap. Barabas triggers our full prejudicial response here by generalizing his good fortune to all Jews; for the nonce, he is representative of his nation, not himself alone: "*We* have scambled up / More wealth by far than those that brag of faith" (120–21). And just as he gets our hostility flowing freely, he exposes its source and shows us for what we are in spite of our faith's "profession":

> Who hateth me but for my happiness?
> Or who is honor'd now but for his wealth?
> Rather had I, a Jew, be hated thus,
> Than pitied in a Christian poverty;
> For I can see no fruits in all their faith,
> But malice, falsehood, and excessive pride,
> Which methinks fits not their profession.
>
> (110–16)

Like Machiavel in the Prologue, Barabas has invited our hisses and then pointed to their hidden motive, in this case, the envy that belies our ostensible Christian sanction for Jew-baiting. Now having turned the spotlight back on us, he can pick out other unwholesome fruits that blossom among our brethren and then weigh the pros and cons of his faith and ours. If we take consolation (or "excessive pride?") in the fact that Christians govern the world in which Jews prosper, Barabas will grant us that and rest content in the "peaceful rule" that wealth (unlike principality) allows him. If we align ourselves with "Christian" governance against the Jew, we are adopting a position that the play will make unflattering. But in any case, this flaunting speech is likely to provoke our antagonism all the more by exposing its ugly roots.

Thus far the antagonism that Barabas provokes in his Christian audience has provided the play's only conflict. But now three of his "countrymen" bring in the news that a Turkish fleet is menacing Malta and that all Jews have been summoned to a meeting in the senate house. In the ensuing dialogue, Barabas falls into what will be his constant habit of knavish, sardonic asides: "Assure yourselves I'll look unto—(*aside*) myself." And when his "brethren" leave, he calls his wits together to size up the situation in a soliloquy that closes the scene and articulates his villainous self-concern: "Howe'er the world go, I'll make sure for one." This recalls not only the manner but the matter of Richard, who was equally "himself alone." But at this point in their respective plays, evident similarities only highlight important differences. For example, the opening scenes are virtually identical structurally. In each the villain-protagonist introduces himself and the situation, has an exchange that goes all his way (Barabas with the two merchants, Richard with Clarence), expresses his self-satisfaction thereupon, is then confronted with worrisome news, and adjusts his strategy accordingly in a concluding soliloquy. Yet the effect on us is altogether different. Whereas we are made to share Richard's ironies with him, we are so set against Barabas by the first sequences that his knavish "confidences" toward the end of the scene can scarcely serve to engage us with him. Though we see his point of view here (as his baffled brethren do not), he shares no joke and no scheme with us. In fact, we may be stung by Barabas's taunts into a less-than-Christian gratification that he is hailed so summarily out of his countinghouse by the Maltese authorities, or be lured into supposing him too naively secure when he brushes aside the apparent threat to his "peaceful rule" (though his final solitary scrutiny of Turkish policy should dampen any such hope). If so, we are picking up the habit of matching wits with Barabas and of measuring ourselves against him that the play will encourage to the end. In any case, we are in the hands of a very different sort of knave than Richard.

Our introduction to Christian governance in Malta plays directly to our political acumen, our ability (already identified in the Prologue as a cardinal Machiavellian principle) to weigh what is said by what is done and *not* to weigh men by their words. Helped by Barabas's assessment of the situation at the end of scene 1, we recognize the diplomatic dance with which the Christians and the Turks open scene 2 for precisely what it is. The naiveté of Ferneze's questions ("Now, bashaws, what demand you at our hands?"), his request for time to consult with his knights (the previous summons of the Jews shows clearly that he had already decided what to do), and the verbal politesse of the Turkish envoys (" 'tis more kingly to obtain by peace / Than to enforce conditions by constraint. . . . Farewell, *great* governors, and *brave* Knights of Malta") glow transparently over the plain fact that the powerful Turks are putting the squeeze on the weaker Maltese. And when Ferneze attempts to keep this graceful sidestep moving as he, in turn, squeezes the Jews of Malta, it is Barabas who gratifies our sense of reality by refusing to dance:

> *Ferneze*:   Hebrews, now come near.
>   From the Emperor of Turkey is arriv'd
>   Great Selim Calymath, his Highness' son,
>   To levy of us ten years' tribute past;
>   Now then, here know that it concerneth us—
> *Barabas*: Then, good my lord, to keep your quiet still,
>   Your lordship shall do well to let them have it.
> *Ferneze*: Soft, Barabas, there's more 'longs to 't than so.
>   To what this ten years' tribute will amount,
>   That we have cast, but cannot compass it
>   By reason of the wars, that robb'd our store;
>   And therefore are we to request your aid.
> *Barabas*: Alas, my lord, we are no soldiers:
>   And what's our aid against so great a prince?
> (2:38–51)

Prodded by this sort of ironic ridicule, extortion bares its ugly head:

>   Tut, Jew, we know thou art no soldier;
>   Thou art a merchant, and a moneyed man,
>   And 'tis thy money, Barabas, we seek.

But once the facts are thus allowed to surface, Ferneze's gestures toward covering them again with a cloak of piety inevitably seem a crude and "palpable device":

> *2 Knight*: Have strangers leave with us to get their wealth?
>   Then let them with us contribute.
> *Barabas*: How, equally?
> *Ferneze*:   No, Jew, like infidels.
>   For through our sufferance of your hateful lives,
>   Who stand accursed in the sight of heaven,
>   These taxes and afflictions are befall'n,
>   And therefore thus we are determined:
>   Read there the articles of our decrees.
> *1 Officer*: (*reading*) First, the tribute money of the Turks

> shall all be levied amongst the Jews, and each of them to
> pay one half of his estate.
> (2:60–70)

As Barabas's irony modulates into outrage through this
sequence, we are maneuvered into sharing his point of view, or at
least made to acknowledge the merit of it, in a way that we can
scarcely have anticipated when he antagonized us in the first
scene. We may have been prepared to enjoy the rich Jew's
discomfiture, but we cannot evade the clear justice and accuracy
of his charges against his Christian persecutors;

> Is theft the ground of your religion?
> .   .   .   .   .
> Your extreme right does me exceeding wrong.
> .   .   .   .   .
> Ay, policy! that's their profession,
> And not simplicity, as they suggest.
> (2:95, 153, 160–61)

Since such a point is made of the "exceeding wrong" done to
Barabas, we could only share the spirit of the triumph over him
here by consciously sharing the Christian (or "Machiavellian")
hypocrisy with which it is accomplished, a hypocrisy made all
the more apparent when the poker-faced Ferneze allows himself
the rare luxury of some ironic mockery of his own:

> If thou rely upon thy righteousness,
> Be patient and thy riches will increase.
> Excess of wealth is cause of covetousness,
> And covetousness, O, 'tis a monstrous sin.
> (2:121–24)

But if we want to rely on our own right-mindedness more than
open allegiance with Ferneze's cynicism would permit us to do,
the confrontation calls on responses that are more gratifying to
us. Barabas had, in the very first exchange here, spoken
winningly to our accurate perception of the situation by
puncturing the governor's rhetorical facade. When the axe first
falls, the contrast between Barabas and his cringing brethren is
again bound to tell to his advantage:

1 Officer: (*reading*) Secondly, he that denies to pay [half
    of his estate], shall straight become a Christian.
Barabas: How! a Christian! Hum, what's here to do?
1st Officer: (*reading*) Lastly, he that denies this, shall
    absolutely lose all he has.
All 3 Jews: O, my lord, we will give half.
Barabas: O, earth-mettl'd villains, and no Hebrews born!
    And will you basely thus submit yourselves
    To leave your goods to their arbitrament?
Ferneze: Why, Barabas, wilt thou be christen'd?
Barabas: No, governor, I will be no convertite.
    (2:73–82)

We need not accept all Barabas's arguments in the ensuing
debate in order to be impressed by the fact that he alone attempts
to stand out against the clear injustice. And when he is singled
out for complete despoilment in reprisal for his bold stand, he
surely seems to have earned the outrage and the grief to which he
gives way. Having already appealed to our "better" side—our in-
telligence, our fairness, our generous admiration for bravery even
in an enemy or alien—Barabas now calls directly for the pity that
is so notably lacking in the Maltese Christians and the sympathy
that seems beyond the small spirits of his simpering "brethren":

And having all, you can request no more,
Unless your unrelenting flinty hearts
Suppress all pity in your stony breasts,
And now shall move you to bereave my life.
    (2:140–43)

O, silly brethren, born to see this day!
Why stand you thus unmov'd with my laments?
Why weep you not to think upon my wrongs?
Why pine not I, and die in this distress?
    (2:170–73)

Whether or not we will feel much actual sympathy for this
grotesque Jew in his "extreme sorrows" is an open question; but
it is easy, and again flattering to our sense of our better selves, to
acknowledge that the poor wretch deserves to be pitied; and the
whole scene has encouraged this easy and conventional (or

"natural") response, which implies our superiority not only to Barabas himself, but to everyone with whom he interacts here.

But having allowed us such satisfaction, Barabas now turns on us with the unkindest cut of all. The outrage and the grief that we may have condescended to pity, and which we in any case have seen to be both justified and sincere, were simply an act! His soliloquy, addressed our way after the three weak-kneed Jews "leave him in his ireful mood," implies our mutual confidentiality, our shared and superior knavish perspective on the whole proceedings in the senate house:

> See the simplicity of these base slaves,
> Who, for the villains have no wit themselves,
> Think me to be a senselesss lump of clay
> That will with every water wash to dirt:
> No, Barabas is born to better chance,
> And fram'd of finer mold than common men,
> That measure naught but by the present time.
> A reaching thought will search his deepest wits,
> And cast with cunning for the time to come:
> For evils are apt to happen every day—
> (2:214–23)

But nothing in this scene has offered us such a perspective. In spite of Barabas's previous resolve to "make sure for one," everything that follows his muttered surprise at the government's terms ("How, a Christian! Hum, what's here to do?" [74–75]) has encouraged us to believe that the wily Jew has actually been caught out and, in his anger and grief, is reaping the bitter consequences. If we have been drawn into generously acknowledging his grievance, then he has made fools of us along with everyone onstage. And his knavish confidentiality after the fact is, therefore, a slap in the face that lumps us with the other simple "base slaves" who have underestimated him. Since we haven't been in on the joke, the whole sequence, with its surprise punch at the end, has just the opposite effect from Richard's early knavery. Instead of making us see and feel the action his way, the boasting Jew insults us in the very process of "confiding" in us. The soliloquy is a practical (as well as verbal) lesson in

Machiavellianism. We learn the hard way not to trust Barabas and not, by all means, to pity him again.[7]

Our surprise at this reversal determines our response to Barabas's own surprise at the next turn, which follows hard upon. While we are still adjusting to the idea that Barabas is one up after all, the "beauteous Abigail" enters and pulls the rug out from under her father's smug assurance with the news that his house, together with the precious hoard he had so providently hidden therein, has already been seized and converted to a nunnery—no male Jews allowed. Only forty lines have passed since Barabas dropped the mask of his false sorrow, and here he is bursting out again:

> My gold, my gold, and all my wealth is gone!
> You partial heavens, have I deserv'd this plague?
> What, will you thus oppose me, luckless stars,
> To make me desperate in my poverty?
> And knowing me impatient in distress
> Think me so mad as I will hang myself,
> That I may vanish o'er the earth in air,
> And leave no memory that e'er I was?
> (2:256–63)

There can be no question that the "tragic" note is sincere now, and the effect for us is inevitably comic. Just as he is boasting to us of his cunning, the Jew falls on his face. The comic pleasure that fall gives us will be heightened to the degree that we were victims of his cunning. Duped as we were by his feigned passion, there is no chance whatever that we will now lend ourselves to the spirit either of his actual grief or of the "heroic" resolve with which Barabas (a specialist in resurrections) determines to rouse himself against the "partial heavens" and "luckless stars." The superiority we should have enjoyed over this Jew from the beginning, that had seemed ours by way of condescension toward his ruin moments ago and then was snatched rudely away by his self-congratulatory soliloquy, is now ours for the having. And we won't let the comfortable detachment of our comic pleasure at Barabas's sudden reversal slip back into any serious investment in his plight. We will sit back, rather, and watch him "sink or swim"—his own terms for his options here.

Barabas rouses himself, in any case, not to heroic defiance of the stars, but to the "shifts" and "policy" of knavery. Had he played the knave *for* us from the beginning, or even through the senate-house sequence, we might by now be engaged into his controlling perspective as he acts his part and directs Abigail through the paces of her "counterfeit profession" so that she may gain admission to their house-turned-nunnery. But he has put us off so effectively that now, when he starts a plot in motion with our full awareness for the first time in the play, we can watch his "shifts" with impartial amusement. There is little in the staging of his scheme, in any event, to catch us up in his knavish sport at the dupes' expense. The straight-faced abbess and her attendant friars do nothing—yet!—that exposes them as targets for our ironic laughter. Nor does Barabas play wittily to our ironic awareness here, as Richard had done so consistently. He is funny but not witty as he shifts abruptly back and forth between his public mask of fatherly wrath and his whispered exhortations to Abigail. Note that these asides express his miserly anxiety, not his knavish glee:

> Nay, back, Abigail.
> (*whispers to her*) And think upon the jewels and the gold;
> The board is marked thus (*makes cross*) that covers it.
> —Away, accursed, from thy father's sight.
> . . . . .
> (*aside to Abigail*) The board is marked thus (*makes cross*)
>   that covers it.
> —For I had rather die, than see her thus.
> Wilt thou forsake me too in my distress,
> Seduced daughter? (*aside to her*) Go, forget not.
> —Becomes it Jews to be so credulous?
> (*aside to her*) Tomorrow early I'll be at the door.
> —No, come not at me, if thou wilt be damn'd.
> Forget me, see me not, and so be gone.
> (*aside [to her]*) Farewell; remember tomorrow morning.
> —Out, out, thou wretch.
> (2:341–58)

As Barabas repeatedly thrusts poor Abigail off and then yanks her back again for another anxious aside, we are bound to laugh;

and such asides make him more the object than the director of our fun.

The detachment Barabas had provoked in us has another important consequence here. On the very heels of the soliloquy in which he has insulted us for trusting his grief, and more sharply for any sympathy we may have condescended to lend him, his daughter Abigail enters and gives herself entirely over to him:

> Not for myself, but aged Barabas:
> Father, for thee lamenteth Abigail.
> (2:228–29)

This selflessness, this capacity for love and sympathy, is a new note in the play, and it is Abigail alone who gives it what precarious life it will ever have in Malta. She might thus provide a focus and an outlet for our better humane feelings, the one warm soul in a cold, hard world. The timing of her entrance, however, works against such a response. At the end of this scene Mathias tells his rival-to-be, Lodowick, that the sight of Abigail would "have mov'd your heart, / Though countermur'd with walls of brass, to love, / Or at the least to pity" (2:378–80). Perhaps, but the play has been constructing just such walls in us from the beginning, and any feelings of love or pity on our part when we first see Abigail will have to come from hearts just countermured by Barabas's brassy soliloquy. In this context, when she gives herself so completely over to her father and his stratagem, we are more likely to condescend to her as the Jew's fool than look up to her as our humane exemplar. We are simply not allowed to watch this play through Abigail's soft eyes.

Barabas's stratagem and its execution are gross and palpable enough to remind us more of Titivillus and his board in *Mankind* than of Richard's witty wooing of Anne. The scheme works nonetheless, and its successful conclusion brings the first action or plot of this play to an end. It is a happy ending for Barabas *and* for us, but there is no shared gratification between us. Ours is all at his expense. As he opens the scene that will bring him his gold and his bliss once more, the Jew is again sounding the tragic knell:

> Thus like the sad presaging raven that tolls
> The sick man's passport in her hollow beak,
> And in the shadow of the silent night
> Doth shake contagion from her sable wings,
> Vex'd and tormented runs poor Barabas
> With fatal curses towards these Christians.
>   . . . . .
> No sleep can fasten on my watchful eyes,
> Nor quiet enter my distemper'd thoughts,
> Till I have answer of my Abigail.
> (2.1.1–19)

No knavish pose this, of course. It is, rather, the exposed anxiety that Richard never allowed us to see until the bitter end. But, even more than in his outburst against the "partial heavens" in the preceding scene, Barabas's tragedy is our comedy. Nothing could amuse us more at this point than the sight of "poor Barabas" running "vex'd and tormented" with thoughts distempered by miserly greed. That his lament (laden as it is with sad presaging ravens and the contagion of night's sable wings) verges on parody makes our amusement all the easier to indulge. Nor does the fact that Abigail appears above as the lodestar of Barabas's life and grants him happiness in the form of his moneybags dampen our pleasure a whit, for Barabas's joy reduces him in our eyes even more effectively than his grief:

> My gold, my fortune, my felicity;
> Strength to my soul, death to mine enemy;
> Welcome, the first beginner of my bliss!
> O, Abigail, that I had thee here too,
> Then my desires were fully satisfied;
> But I will practice thy enlargement thence.
> O girl, O gold, O beauty, O my bliss! *Hugs his bags*
> (48–54)

Rather than the commanding Jew who surprised and offended us in the first scene or the wily Jew who fooled and insulted us in the second, we now finally have what we expected but did not get at the beginning: the caricature Jew "who smiles to see how full his bags are cramm'd." And we smile too. We have him where we want him now, and the superiority we enjoy over him here is all the sweeter for the setbacks we have endured at the hands of this peculiar knave.

In effect, the play starts anew after Barabas's rapturous recovery from Ferneze's golden fleecing.[8] As the Maltese form a "holy alliance" against the "barbarous misbelieving Turks," the political overplot goes its separate (and significantly different) way from the main line of action, which is now controlled completely by Barabas's knavish villainy. Barabas starts this new sequence in the characteristic manner of the confidential knave, introducing us to the scene and his stance in it as though this were in fact the beginning of the play. But if he is now master of the action that he both presents and directs, and if that action is now played primarily for our amusement, we nevertheless continue to enjoy Barabas and his show from the superior perspective he afforded us in his miserly ecstasy. Several things allow us to place this knave's antics as a sort of theatrical entertainment that we neither take very seriously nor share in his own spirit.

For one thing, Barabas's keynote remains his alien Jewishness, which may no longer be so threatening to us now that it descends into caricature villainy (we were likely to be more offended by his legitimate success in the first scene than we will be by his mass murders!), but which he continues to hurl in our faces in an abrasive way. His confidential introduction to us in his "new" role as villain invites our disdain in ways that distinguish it from other knaves' presentations of their credentials:

> We Jews can fawn like spaniels when we please,
> And when we grin, we bite; yet are our looks
> As innocent and harmless as a lamb's.
> I learn'd in Florence how to kiss my hand,
> Heave up my shoulders when they call me dog,
> And duck as low as any barefoot friar,
> Hoping to see them starve upon a stall,
> Or else be gather'd for in our synagogue,

> That when the offering basin comes to me,
> Even for charity I may spit into 't.
> (2.3.20–29)

Contrast the effect of this with Richard's similar declaration in *3 Henry VI*:

> Why, I can smile, and murder whiles I smile,
> And cry "Content!" to that which grieves my heart,
> And wet my cheeks with artificial tears,
> And frame my face to all occasions.
> I'll drown more sailors than the mermaid shall;
> I'll slay more gazers than the basilisk;
> I'll play the orator as well as Nestor,
> Deceive more slily than Ulysses could
> And, like a Sinon, take another Troy.
> I can add colors to the chameleon,
> Change shapes with Proteus for advantages,
> And set the murderous Machiavel to school.
> Can I do this, and cannot get a crown?
> Tut, were it farther off, I'll pluck it down.
> (3.2.182–95)

That's not a very nice thing to say either; but what a difference in the way it is said! Since it is straight exposition, it doesn't actually involve us in Richard's point of view, as many of the ironies we share with him in *Richard III* do. But it *is* an engaging speech. The positive delight in the list of skills virtually demands that the actor show them off for us in the process of stating them through the first few lines. And from the smile at the beginning through the self-consciously grandiose prophecies to the cavalier esprit of the final line, all is done with a good humor that helps to make this a *winning* performance.

Whereas Richard soars over all mythic models as "himself alone" ("I'll drown *more* sailors than the mermaid shall; / I'll slay *more* gazers than the basilisk"), Barabas insists that he represents the despised stereotype ("*We* Jews can fawn"). As with Richard, the actor is encouraged to mime the poses Barabas describes, but they are all demeaning ones. He fawns, cringes, and grovels—tricks he learned in the Florentine school whose murderous master Richard had demoted to a mere novice. And the spiteful nastiness of "hoping to see them starve upon a stall" looks all the more petty when it is set over against Richard's grand design. Barabas has hissed and spit his way through the speech from first ("In spite of these swine-eating Christians") to last ("even for charity I may spit into 't"); so it is altogether fitting that when he openly assumes the knave's mantle in his next speech, it bears the crest of the serpent (2.3.36–37). His later "blessing" over the poisoned pottage he sends to his daughter and the nuns is sealed with the same venomous signet:

> In few, the blood of Hydra, Lerna's bane,
> The juice of hebon, and Cocytus' breath,
> And all the poisons of the Stygian pool
> Break from the fiery kingdom, and in this
> Vomit your venom, and envenom her
> That like a fiend hath left her father thus.
> (3.4.95–100)

If he is so nasty and so noxious, how can we be amused by Barabas and his villainy? Partly because he is *so* nasty and *so* noxious, of course: "The Villain" in a stagy way that makes him both easy to hiss and easy to enjoy. His verbal venom swells until it overflows into burlesque. As with his "tragic" outbursts of miserly grief in the earlier night scene (act 2, scene 1), we can relax and smile even while we "shudder" at the terrible Jew who is now reduced to such readily recognizable caricature, though the contours of the legendary well-poisoner now come into much sharper relief than those of the gold-hugger:

> As for myself, I walk abroad a' nights
> And kill sick people groaning under walls;
> Sometimes I go about and poison wells;
> And now and then, to cherish Christian thieves,
> *I am content to lose some of my crowns,*
> That I may, walking in my gallery,
> See 'em go pinion'd along by my door.
> (2.3.175–81; my italics)

The point here, of course, as when he later refuses to let the loss of a ship spoil the pleasure of his scheme to kill Lodowick, is not

that Barabas loves money less, but that he loves murder more
(2.3.244–51). And neither he nor anyone else allows us to forget
for a moment that his villainy is as true to his Jewish stereotype
as his greed:

> And like a cunning Jew so cast about . . .
> (2.3.236)

> Then, like a Jew, he laugh'd and jeer'd . . .
> (4.2.106)

He is playing his part for us just as he should now.

Ithamore, the "trusty Turk" whom Barabas buys in the bargain
basement of the slave market, highlights both the nasty and the
funny colors in the Jew's knavery through the middle sequences
of the play. On the one hand, the knavish purity of Ithamore's
addiction to the "sport" of villainy sets off the malice of his
master's "spite." But at the same time, when the flow of Barabas's
malice might otherwise simply disgust us, Ithamore makes sure
that we laugh, as when his "innocent" admiration keeps us from
gagging on the curse that Barabas spews out over the poisoned
pot of rice: "What a blessing has he giv'n 't! Was ever pot of rice
porridge so sauc'd?" And though Barabas can hyperbolize
villainy into absurd proportions all on his own, Ithamore
consistently manages to broaden and thus lighten the comic
effect. If the extravagant list of atrocities in the curriculum vitae
with which Barabas dazzles his new protégé fails to get us
grinning, the eagerness to please in Ithamore's response will
surely do the trick:

> *Barabas*: Being young, I studied physic, and began
>   To practice first upon the Italian;
>   There I enrich'd the priests with burials,
>   And always kept the sexton's arms in ure
>   With digging graves and ringing dead men's knells.
>   And after that was I an engineer,
>   And in the wars 'twixt France and Germany,
>   Under pretense of helping Charles the Fifth,
>   Slew friend and enemy with my stratagems.
>   Then after that was I an usurer,

And with extorting, cozening, forfeiting,
And tricks belonging unto brokery,
I fill'd the jails with bankrouts in a year,
And with young orphans planted hospitals,
And every moon made some or other mad,
And now and then one hang himself for grief,
Pinning upon his breast a long great scroll,
How I with interest tormented him.

. . . . .

But tell me, now, how hast thou spent thy time?
Ithamore: Faith, master,
In setting Christian villages on fire,
Chaining of eunuchs, binding galley slaves.
One time I was an hostler in an inn,
And in the nighttime secretly would I steal
To travelers' chambers, and there cut their throats.
Once at Jerusalem, where the pilgrims kneel'd,
I strowed powder on the marble stones,
And therewithal their knees would rankle, so
That I have laugh'd a-good to see the cripples
Go limping home to Christendom on stilts.
Barabas: Why, this is something!
(2.3.182–214)

Barabas has a mordant wit that is beyond the simpler reach of Ithamore's blithe spirit, and we still feel its troublesome bite now and then ("It's no sin to deceive a Christian, / For they themselves hold it a principle / Faith is not to be held with heretics" [2.3.310–12]). But while he is teamed with Ithamore he is rendered mostly harmless (to *us*) through comic reduction that makes him as much the butt as the provider of our laughter.[9] True, while the team lasts, Barabas maintains his superiority as master more surely and entirely than some other knaves manage to do over their servant-accomplices (we will note Volpone's problems in this regard later on). The schemes and the direction of them are almost exclusively his—Ithamore virtually asks permission to add a touch of his own in the hilarious routine of the friar who "kills" his dead rival's propped-up corpse. And in the unlikely case that we might take Barabas's professed "adoption" of Ithamore straight, he assures us in two brief soliloquies that he has his villainous wits about him (3.4.50–52, 111). Since these confidences to us come after the fact, it is possible that he remains for a few moments (as had been his way earlier) one up on us as well as on his "trusty Ithamore." But such a surprise (if it is one) need scarcely ruffle the general condescension we can now maintain toward him when the latter is so consistently reinforced by the very terms in which Ithamore "admires" Barabas's knavish mastery, terms that merge the Vice's customary mockery of the bottle-nosed devil with the inevitable joke on the Jew:

> O brave, master; I worship your nose for this.
> (2.3.174)

> O, mistress! I have the bravest, gravest, secret, subtle,
> bottle-nos'd knave to my master that ever gentleman had.
> (3.3.9–10)

For the most part, Barabas's bustling knavery deserves to be admired at just such a comically deflated rate. "See . . . / How *busy* Barabas is there above / To entertain us," says Calymath as he enters in the final scene (51–53), and that is the primary effect that the Jew's several contrivances have on us. Whereas in the opening scene he surprised us with the masterful ease of his apparent control over the vast Mediterranean seaways, now we are impressed by the excessive energy he invests in patently simple "plots." Neither setting Abigail's suitors (and later the friars) at self-destructive odds nor poisoning the nuns' rice requires any remarkable ingenuity; so when we are asked to marvel at the performance ("Why, was there ever seen such villainy, / So neatly plotted, and so well performed?" [3.3.1–2]), we won't respond in kind, as we do when Richard puts this sort of question to us ("Was ever woman in this humor wooed?" [1.2.227]). Successful knavery always depends on our awareness of its theatricality, of course, but at its most engaging it makes us appreciate the wit with which the knave contrives and carries off his show. The disparity in Barabas's case between the simplicity of his knavish plots and the extravagance of his knavish pose focuses our amusement on the latter. We can delight in the artistry of Richard's show, but we smile at the extremity of Barabas's showiness. Admittedly, the distinction is not quite so absolute. Just as Richard at his least winning could fall into mechanical asides "like the formal Vice, Iniquity" (3.1.82), so Barabas can manage an occasional irony for us to share in the manner of Richard's best "piety": "This is mere frailty, brethren; be content" (4.1.97). But most of Barabas's scheming is conducted with such a flurry of explanatory asides and such an elaborate shuffling back and forth between dupes who are only too willing to be moved about like wooden pawns that we are more amused by the "busyness" of his knavery than by its wit. He "acts" his villainy in a manner that is as hyperbolically stagy as his description of it to Ithamore had been.

We would, in any case, notice the self-consciously theatrical mode of Barabas's knavery. But our tendency to place it as "mere" theatrics, and thus to reduce it to the realm of harmless entertainment, depends partly on the very different kind of understanding that Ferneze and the political overplot require of us. The "theater" in which Richard enacts his plots includes the entire world of his play, even when that world is beyond his control. Bosworth field is recognizably on the same stage as the street where Richard wooed Anne or the Tower where Clarence was murdered. But when Barabas commences his role as villain in act 2, scene 3, the council house where Ferneze conducts his very different brand of policy remains, in effect, apart from the Jew's overtly theatrical stage. In the two brief scenes in which Ferneze first allies himself with the Spaniards (act 2, scene 2) and then defies the Turks (act 3, scene 5), there are no confidential asides or soliloquies, no villainous leers or wicked smiles, no propped-up friar's corpses or poisoned pots, and no indecorous jokes—none of the things, that is, that make the antics of Barabas and Ithamore so pointedly theatrical.

This is not to say that we take the dialogue of the "grave governor" at its own straight-faced value. Unlike the first scene in the council house, however, where Barabas forced both Ferneze's hand and our recognition of it, we must now rely entirely on our own shrewdness to penetrate the diplomatic smokescreen. There are enough signals to be sure that we do so, unless we are simply too obtuse to be a fit audience for Marlowe's play. The grand line with which Ferneze caps the scene of his new Spanish alliance, for example—"Honor is bought with blood and not with gold" (2.2.56)—scarcely conceals the solid financial basis that the money just extorted from the Jews provides for this glorious war:

> *1 Knight*: Del Bosco, as thou lovest and honor'st us,
> Persuade our governor against the Turk.
> This truce we have is but in hope of gold,
> *And with that sum he craves might we wage war.*
> (24–27; my italics)

Just how the Spaniard "loves and honors" his new allies is clear from the way he has muscled his way onto their island uninvited to reap the profit of his Turkish captives in the Maltese slave market (3, 9–18), and clearer still from the terms in which he gives Malta the "freedom" to take on new Spanish overlords:

> My lord and king hath title to this isle,
> And he means quickly to expel you hence;
> Therefore be rul'd by me [!], and keep the gold.
> I'll write unto his Majesty for aid
> And not depart until I see you free.
> (37–41)

Seeing how the cards are now stacked, Ferneze grants Del Bosco the lucrative "condition" he seeks ("On this condition shall thy Turks be sold" [42]) and offers his absent Turkish foe some suitably defiant rhetoric to close the scene.

What are the consequences of seeing Ferneze's world this way? The critical reader concentrating on thematic parallels is likely to stress the leveling effect that reveals the solemn governor and the grotesque Jew as brothers under the skin—politicians both, who use similarly deceptive means to self-serving ends in a world where "the wind that bloweth all" is "desire of gold" (3.5.3–4) and where "every one's price," be he slave or statesman, "is written on his back" (2.3.3). Such a reading, which can lead to a single satiric judgment on the whole sordid world of the play, has much to support it, including Barabas's charge (not to be refuted on evidence from the play itself) that his Christian antagonists are as "bad" as he is:

> Thus, loving neither, will I live with both,
> Making a profit of my policy;
> And he from whom my most advantage comes
> Shall be my friend.
> This is the life we Jews are us'd to lead;
> And reason, too, for Christians do the like.[10]
> (5.2.111–16)

But to say simply that Barabas and Ferneze "do the like" because each pursues his own "most advantage" is to ignore the radically different ways we are made to see them do so and the consequent discriminations in which we are implicated as an audience through the middle sequences of the play. There *is* a "difference of things" in Malta, though it is not the moral one that poor, foolish Abigail thinks she sees when she returns to the Christian fold (3.3.59–65).

Neither plot line, in any case, plays to our moral judgment. In Barabas's underworld we are made to laugh at villainy and its victims alike, made effectively "void" of the "affections" of compassion and love that have no place here, and made to "smile when the Christians moan," as Barabas would have his eager apprentice Ithamore do (2.3.170–73). We might excuse our callous amusement on the grounds that the papish Christians we see, those "religious caterpillars" (4.1.20), are so grossly undeserving of our compassion as they stumble over their own greed into Barabas's knavish snare. But in fact we are made to laugh just as heartily at innocent Abigail's death, which the erstwhile sober Friar Barnardine turns into a bawdy joke (3.6.41). The only sort of judgment we are really asked to make through these scenes is a worldly wise one against the fools' credulity (Barabas appropriately damns Abigail for being "credulous" [3.4.24]):

> But are not both these wise men to suppose
> That I will leave my house, my goods, and all,
> To fast and be well whipp'd?

And, like everything else in this overexposed phase of Barabas's knavery, the sardonic answer is handed directly to us: "I'll none of that" (4.1.121–23).

The real distinction between the Jew and the governor, then, is not a matter of morality but of theatrical mode. Set against Barabas's stagecraft, which appeals so openly to our sense of theater, Ferneze's careful statecraft calls inevitably on our sense of reality: this, we recognize, is how *actual* policy works. To say that this discrimination makes us more condescending toward Barabas and his knavery is not to say that we consciously approve of Ferneze's "unseen hypocrisy" more than we do of the Jew's "counterfeit profession" (1.2.290–91). But our very capacity to *understand* Ferneze's political world without any explanatory asides inevitably reduces Barabas's ostentatious villainy by comparison to something less "serious," less challenging and more entertaining. The "difference of things," as we sense them in the play (whether we articulate the distinction or not), is between a politician whose use of realpolitik we credit and a stage Machiavel whose antics we enjoy, between the intellectual demands of what we take to be a mirror of reality and the easier pleasures of that which we place as fiction.

Through the long middle section of the play we can give these contrasting modes the very different kinds of interest they evoke without getting involved in any issues joined between the politic governor and the knavish Jew. Their clash in the second scene had forced attention to the moral implications of Ferneze's "pious" extortion:

> *Ferneze*: Excess of wealth is cause of covetousness,
>   And covetousness, O, 'tis a monstrous sin.
> *Barabas*: Ay, but theft is worse; tush, take not from me then,
>   For that is theft.
> . . . . .
> *Ferneze*: Content thee, Barabas; thou hast naught but right.
> *Barabas*: Your extreme right does me exceeding wrong.
> (1.2.123–53)

Right and wrong were very much at stake there in a way that disturbed the basis of our own original antagonism to the Jew. And when Barabas begins his new stage life as a villain in act 2, scene 3, his professed motive of revenge against Ferneze and his son promises to keep this apparently central conflict and the issue of respective "wrongs" (if not rights) alive for us in the play.

Occasionally, early in the new action, that issue rises tauntingly out of the profusion of sneering asides and grimaces with which Barabas manages the duping of Lodowick:

> *Barabas*: Good sir,
> Your father has deserv'd it [a gift] at my hands,
> Who, of mere charity and Christian ruth,
> To bring me to religious purity,
> And, as it were, in catechizing sort,
> To make me mindful of my mortal sins,
> Against my will, and whether I would or no,
> Seiz'd all I had, and thrust me out a' doors,
> And made my house a place for nuns most chaste.
> *Lodowick*: No doubt your soul shall reap the fruit of it.
> (2.3.70–79).

Like father like son, apparently. But Barabas and Ferneze never meet on this ground again. Indeed, they don't meet at all between the second scene and the fifth act — some four-fifths of the play. In the long interim, Ferneze makes only one brief appearance in Barabas's main line of action in order to mourn his murdered son. It is, for Ferneze, an uncharacteristically "theatrical" appearance, in the manner of Hieronimo:

> O, that my sighs could turn to lively breath,
> And these my tears to blood, that he might live.
> (3.2.18–19)

It may be significant that Ferneze adopts so easily the appropriate hyperbolic mode when he enters Barabas's "play," whereas Barabas later cannot manage successfully the shift into Ferneze's political world. In any case, after this one tragic outburst, Ferneze goes back to the "real" business of governing Malta that is his proper concern. Nor does Barabas intrude, during this part of the play, into the council house. As the murder of Lodowick leads him to the murder of Abigail, and that in turn to the murder of the friars, and all these prepare the way for Ithamore's defection to the cuddly camp of Bellamira, Barabas loses sight of Ferneze and we lose sight of the moral issue that had been posed between them. Seeing them only in their separate spheres, we are impressed instead by their contrasting modes, and the issue of

"Christian wrong" is reduced to "saucy" jokes about frisky friars and naughty nuns in the comic world of Barabas's knavery, where it can be easily laughed at and laughed off.

Since Barabas's line of action is so much more amusing than Ferneze's, we enjoy the large space given it as it grows more and more comic and moves further and further away from the severe concerns of the "grave governor." As a team, Barabas and Ithamore are at their knavish best in their third and last success: the farce of the friars. And they are even funnier when the rival team of Pilia-Borza and Bellamira turn the "trusty Turk" against his master. Who would have dreamed, when the powerful Jew addressed us from his countinghouse in the opening scene, that we would ever have the smug pleasure of watching him sneak into Bellamira's musky lair disguised as a French musician and armed against *this* sea of troubles with a cartoon accent ("Must tuna my lute for sound, twang, twang" [4.4.29]) and a poisoned posy? But we have long since laughed away the haughty grandeur of "infinite riches in a little room." And when the ludicrously attired Barabas tries vainly to claim back that potent image here in a series of defensive asides, we laugh all the harder:

> *Ithamore*: 'Tis a strange thing of that Jew, he lives upon pickled grasshoppers, and sauc'd mushrooms.
> *Barabas (aside)*: What a slave's this! The governor feeds not as I do.
> *Ithamore*: He never put on clean shirt since he was circumcis'd.
> *Barabas (aside)*: O, rascal! I change myself twice a day.
> *Ithamore*: The hat he wears, Judas left under the elder when he hang'd himself.
> *Barabas (aside)*: 'Twas sent me for a present from the Great Cham.
> *Pilia-Borza*: A masty slave he is. Whither now, fiddler?
> *Barabas*: *Pardona moy,* monsieur, me be no well. *Exit.*
> (4.4.58–67)

We will scarcely recall, as Barabas beats this ignominious retreat under the verbal fire of a "shag-rag knave," that he had originally aimed his vengeance at the governor's cold heart (2.3.16). The two are worlds apart now.

So it seems, indeed, when the two plots are abruptly thrust back together in the following scene (act 5, scene 1). Ferneze, soberly involved with the impending Turkish siege, can hardly believe it when these underworld types dare to interrupt the pressing affairs of state: "Away with her, she is a courtesan" (8). And when Bellamira and her shabby partner persist in blurting out the news of Barabas's various murders, Ferneze's treatment of the Jew is summarily curt. There is no clash between the fell incensed points of mighty opposites. Barabas is haled into court and then off to prison by the scruff of the neck. The issue of Christian policy versus Jewish wealth, debated so strenuously for a hundred lines in their first encounter, is evidently as dead as Barabas's several victims. There *is* no issue here. Barabas, the supervillain in his own show, shrinks to a petty criminal in the clutches of Ferneze's stern authority. The whole exchange takes less than twenty-five lines, the last of which Barabas uses to spit out his apparently futile defiance as he is dragged off: "Devils, do your worst! I live in spite of you!" (41).

And now the play springs another of its surprises on us. The Jew is no sooner out of sight than an officer appears with the announcement that he is dead. Even the imperturbable Ferneze is momentarily taken aback:

> *Ferneze*: Dead?
> *1 Officer*: Dead, my lord, and here they bring his body.
> *Del Bosco*: This sudden death of his is very strange.
> (5.1.52–54)

But the governor's calculating mind has no room in it for the "strange." He quickly naturalizes this turn of events with his convenient piety ("Wonder not at it, sir, the heavens are just"), dismisses the whole sordid business from his thoughts ("Think not of 'em"), disposes of the Jew's body "o'er the walls, / To be a prey for vultures and wild beasts," and, for all we yet know, ends the Jew's play by turning back to the serious work of securing the town.

Is *this* the promised end? If it were, it would be both "very strange" and not so strange at all, depending on which of the two perspectives offered by the play we might use to place it. On the one hand, that Barabas should be so easily dispatched as a nasty nuisance accords with the fact that we no longer take his stage tricks seriously alongside Ferneze's "real" statecraft. On the other, Barabas's exuberant stagecraft has accustomed us to more entertaining spectacles than this drab "ending." But it turns out, of course, not to be the end at all. Barabas more than matches our theatrical expectations of him by pulling the stagiest trick of all. He comes "back to life" and goes on with the show.[11]

It is, however, a different kind of show, or, rather, the two incongruous kinds of shows we have been watching converge. Instead of continuing their separate—even opposite—ways, Barabas's stagecraft and Ferneze's statecraft now meet head on. We can no longer give each its distinctive due in alternate scenes. We must now respond to each more directly in terms of the other, as Barabas tries to convert Ferneze's solid political arena into his own garish brand of theater.

There is, to be sure, nothing particularly new in the soliloquy with which Barabas assures us that he was down but not out:

> What, all alone? well fare, sleepy drink.
> I'll be reveng'd on this accursed town,
> For by my means Calymath shall enter in.
> I'll help to slay their children and their wives,
> To fire the churches, pull their houses down.
> Take my goods, too, and seize upon my lands;
> I hope to see the governor a slave,
> And, rowing in a galley, whipp'd to death.
> (5.1.61–68)

That sounds like good old Bad Barabas, the villain we have loved to hate, at his well-poisoning worst, just as he had introduced himself to Ithamore. But the ease with which he then slips in through the sewer and conquers the town jars the sense of reality that has been given to the Maltese preparations for war, with their careful logistics, thus far in the play. To use the terms of Machiavel's Prologue, can "a childish toy" actually vanquish "a strong-built citadel"? What unsettles us more, perhaps, than the unexpected suddenness with which Barabas replaces Ferneze as governor of Malta, is the feeling that the groundwork of the play has shifted. Barabas's stagy knavery has been allowed to invade Ferneze's hitherto separate sphere of "real" policy. Even Calymath, the beneficiary of the shift, can scarcely credit this theatrical "reversal" in his substantial world of munitions and fortifications:

> And now I see the situation,
> And how secure this conquer'd island stands,
> Environ'd with the Mediterranean Sea,
> Strong countermur'd with other petty isles,
> And toward Calabria, back'd by Sicily
> (Where Syracusian Dionysius reign'd),
> Two lofty turrets that command the town,
> *I wonder how it could be conquer'd thus.*
> (5.3.5–12; my italics)

Calymath, however, isn't inclined to look a gift horse in the nose. He dresses his odd ally in all the proper dignity of the governorship, using the customary diplomatic language of the Maltese council house:

> And, Barabas, as erst we promis'd thee,
> For thy desert we make thee governor;
> . . . . . .
> 'Tis our command; and, Barabas, we give
> To guard thy person, these our Janizaries:
> . . . . . .
> Farewell, brave Jew; farewell, great Barabas.
> (5.2.9–20)

It is Barabas who betrays peculiar signs of uncertainty as he contemplates his new and unaccustomed role, one that he had first discounted as beyond his mercantile reach even at its most powerful (1.1.127–33) and one that his purely destructive villainy (again unlike Richard's) had never aspired to:

> I now am governor of Malta. True,
> But Malta hates me, and in hating me
> My life's in danger, and what boots it thee,
> Poor Barabas, to be the governor,
> Whenas thy life shall be at their command?
> No, Barabas, this must be look'd into;

> And since by wrong thou gott'st authority,
> Maintain it bravely by firm policy;
> At least unprofitably lose it not.
> (5.2.29–37)

Barabas's solitary reliance on "policy" (rather than on Calymath's burly Janizaries) to maintain himself seems characteristic still, and surely his habit of soliloquy continues to distinguish him from Ferneze, who never in his tenure as governor spoke a private word our way. But the gist of this soliloquy and of the subsequent exchange with Ferneze is perplexing to an audience for whom Barabas had become so thoroughly entertaining as a theatrical knave. For one thing, he seems to be changing his own terms to suit the mode of his new role. His concern about maintaining authority over hostile subjects is straight out of *The Prince,* but has no place at all in the lurid policy of the caricature villain's single-minded malice. "I'll help to slay their children and their wives, / To fire the churches, pull their houses down" (5.1.64– 65)—*that* had been the stage Machiavel's proper note. How far it contradicts actual Machiavellian policy as we understand it outside the theater (whether from *The Prince* or from experience and common sense) is acknowledged by "governor" Barabas's rhetorical question to Ferneze:

> And as for Malta's ruin, think you not
> 'Twere slender policy for Barabas
> To dispossess himself of such a place?[12]
> (5.2.64–66)

But if Barabas is in fact adapting his knavery to statecraft rather than stagecraft here, we must also wonder if his new policy is as "slender" as it seems. It looks foolish indeed for him to dispossess himself of his hold over Malta so lightly when he offers to free the city for Ferneze in return for "great sums of money" (76–89), and doubly foolish to allow his hated foe such ample freedom and such full knowledge of his stratagem when he sends Ferneze off to collect those sums from his Christian friends. Can he be so blind? Is he mistaking simple knavery for real policy? Does he suppose that he can dangle Malta before a dazzled Ferneze as he dangled the keys to his vault before

Ithamore and send him ambling off, rich in gullible hope (cf. 3.4.50)? Or does Barabas once again have a trick up his sleeve that, for all his confidentiality, he won't let us in on until after the fact, as was the case in his first "dispossession" (act 1, scene 2), in his apparent adoption of Ithamore (3.4.13–40), and in his feigned death in Ferneze's prison (5.1.80–82)? He hints at such hidden springes when he congratulates himself on his conduct of "the business" after Ferneze leaves:

> My policy detests prevention.
> To what event my secret purpose drives,
> I know; and they shall witness with their lives.
> (5.2.121–23)

Is this the overweening boast of an *alazon* who is now playing his villain's game in the wrong league? Where this sometimes secretive and incredibly resilient knave is concerned, we can't yet be sure.

Given his record for resurrections, we may not even be quite sure, when Barabas finally falls into his own trap, that this is *the* end for him until he himself concedes the point and resolves to die in proper villainous style:

> Then, Barabas, breathe forth thy latest fate,
> And in the fury of thy torments, strive
> To end thy life with resolution.
> Know, governor, 'twas I that slew thy son;
> I fram'd the challenge that did make them meet.
> Know, Calymath, I aim'd thy overthrow,
> And had I but escap'd this stratagem,
> I would have brought confusion on you all,
> Damn'd Christians, dogs, and Turkish infidels.
> But now begins the extremity of heat
> To pinch me with intolerable pangs:
> Die, life! fly, soul! tongue, curse thy fill and die!
>   (*Dies*)
>
> (5.5.77–88)

But by the time Ferneze cuts Barabas's cord, the rules of the very different games these two foes are playing against one another have again come into clear focus in a way that gratifies both our sense of reality *and* our sense of theater. And it is this distinction, jumbled though it may momentarily have been by Barabas's brief succession to the statesman's chair, that stands out finally over whatever point Barabas's insistence on the fundamental likeness between the two parties may carry ("This is the life we Jews are us'd to lead; / And reason, too, for Christians do the like" [5.2.115–16]). Yes, Ferneze also looks to his own "most advantage" and makes a profit of his policy; and yes, Ferneze's "betrayal" of Barabas's last scheme verifies the charge that Christians set Jews a precedent for breaking faith (2.3.310–12). But our strongest impression of Ferneze and Barabas, confirmed more than ever by their conclusive showdown, is of their radical difference in kind, not their likeness. Any supposition that Barabas may have been adopting (though rather badly) the governor's style along with his office is totally dispelled when we see Ferneze's careful counterplot sharply juxtaposed to Barabas's final stratagem, with all its cords and pulleys characteristically showing. First Ferneze, with the efficient brevity that is the soul of his wit, sets down precise guidelines for his well-armed followers:

> In this, my countrymen, be rul'd by me.
> Have special care that no man sally forth
> Till you shall hear a culverin discharg'd
> By him that bears the linstock, kindled thus.
> (5.4.1–4)

And then Barabas appears "with a hammer above, very busy" surrounded not by soldiers but by carpenters. He is as careful here as Ferneze ("Leave nothing loose, all level'd to my mind" [5.5.3]), but all his elaborate preparations are going into the construction of a stage on which he will act his last scene. Only he could have contrived this spectacular finale for us, a theatrical coup that more than makes up for the anticlimactic moment in act 5, scene 1, when flat Ferneze had left both Barabas and the play apparently dead. But Ferneze is content to let Barabas have the show; he will settle for the governorship. His single aside in the entire play is a quiet and condescending appreciation of the Jew's closing performance:

Calymath: Come, my companion bashaws, see, I pray,
How busy Barabas is there above
To entertain us in his gallery.
Let us salute him. Save thee, Barabas.
Barabas: Welcome, great Calymath.
Ferneze (aside): How the slave jeers at him!
(5.5.51–56)

And when Barabas's "counterfeit profession" has run its theatrically inevitable course, Ferneze's "unseen hypocrisy" remains in absolute control. There is no knavish glee whatsoever in his triumph; he is the grave governor still:

So march away, and let due praise be given
Neither to fate nor fortune, but to heaven.
(5.5.122–23)

This refusal to tip us a wink makes Ferneze theatrically unattractive, but politically perfect. Barabas's showmanlike compulsion to reveal all and to take his bows ("And, governor, now partake my policy" [5.5.24]) is what lands him in a boiling cauldron. We know the difference between the showman and the statesman, and weigh the antagonists accordingly—weigh, for example, Ferneze's final curt refusal to allow his valuable hostage out of his clutches ("Content thee, Calymath; here thou must stay, / And live in Malta prisoner" [5.5.117–18]) against Barabas's fatal liberality with Ferneze himself in an identical situation (5.2.91–92). It is to this knowledge and to this judgment that Barabas exposes himself in a direct address to us after we have just seen him place the engine of his own destruction right in Ferneze's sure hands:

Why, is not this
A kingly kind of trade, to purchase towns
By treachery, and sell 'em by deceit?
Now tell me, worldlings, underneath the sun,
If greater falsehood ever has been done?
(5.5.46–50)

Of course that *is* a kingly sort of trade, but not one in which Barabas's stagy "falsehood" can successfully engage.

As worldlings we can turn thumbs down to the absurd "policy" of his elaborate device at the same time that we fully appreciate the grand splash he is about to take for our theatrical pleasure.[13] The distinction we make here between the way of the world and the way of the theater, which allows us our sense of superiority over Barabas in his apparent confusion of the two, also implicates us in Ferneze's own condescension toward Barabas's show, though as an audience we can enjoy that show more overtly than the governor permits himself to do. Bottle-nosed villains are for laughs after all; and by thus gracing the Jew as he deserves, we confirm our own place in the hard-nosed world to which Machiavel had first introduced us, where "there is no sin but ignorance."[14]

3

Volpone

THE CHIMERA OF FOX AND FOOL

"Look, see, see, see!" So Volpone exhorts us and exults to himself
as his would-be heirs find their carefully cultivated hopes dashed
to pieces (5.3.17). It is, of course, essential to the knave's control
over our point of view that we both "see the business" and delight
in his contrivance of it with him, as Volpone asks us to do here.
We watch and laugh with the fox while Mosca, skillfully playing
the role his master has assigned him, drives the greedy gulls to
distraction. But our perspective is more complex than this, since
we also doubt (as Volpone himself does not) the magnifico's control over his parasite's role. Jonson has set us watching the interplay between these two from the very beginning in a way that
modifies our engagement in their knavery even when they are at
their most winning. Volpone is foxy, to be sure, and we enjoy his
craft; but we have seen more than he does, so we are not surprised (as he is) when Mosca finally catches him "out on his hole"
and attempts to turn the erring fox into a complete ass (5.5.7). If
that transformation proves after all to be beyond Mosca's art, he
nonetheless forces Volpone to expose himself publicly for what
we have sensed him to be all along: neither pure fox nor simple
ass, but "a chimera of . . . fool and knave" (5.12.91).[1]

It is this heightened perspective, this consistent distance from
which we enjoy the knaves' games, win or lose, that distinguishes
our view of this play. We experience neither Richard III's movement from engagement to detachment nor the more intense and
volatile interaction that Marlowe provokes with Barabas. Instead,
Jonson makes observant "understanders" of us throughout. "Ob-

servation" is a key term for all the would-be winners in the play, but it is most often used in ways that subject the onstage observers to our superior ironic view. And for the first time since he experimented with comical satire in *Every Man Out of His Humour,* Jonson credits our capacity to maintain our keener perspective over the main action without the expository aid of an onstage commentator. As knave and fool plot their respective ways to their mutual catastrophe, we are stationed high and aloof where our interest and amusement are as safe from the fox's black jaw as from the dull ass's hoof. From that elevation, the final "mortifying of a fox" looks comically appropriate, though the official judgment passed on him may seem, as Jonson acknowledged, rather more severe than this "quick comedy" has promised.[2]

Our more detached perspective begins with Volpone's opening hymn to his gold, which neither engages us into a knavish plot in Richard's immediate way nor goads our not-so-Christian envy, as had Barabas's cool introductory tabulation of *his* "infinite riches in a little room." Instead, Volpone's first speech focuses our attention more on the glittering object he describes and the general behavior it controls than on himself.

> Dear saint,
> Riches, the dumb god that giv'st all men tongues,
> That canst do nought, and yet mak'st men do all things;
> The price of souls; even hell, with thee to boot,
> Is made worth heaven! Thou art virtue, fame,
> Honor, and all things else. Who can get thee,
> He shall be noble, valiant, honest, wise—
> (21–27)

The strong satiric thrust outward toward a world given over to greed competes here for our interest with whatever fascination (surely not engagement) the almost erotic ecstasy of Volpone's worship gains for the speaker himself. At this point, Mosca's summary interruption of his master's trance ("And what he will, sir") spares us a full catalog of gold's limitless transforming powers and diverts Volpone into his first claim to knavery:

> Yet, I glory
> More in the cunning purchase of my wealth
> Than in the glad possession, since I gain
> No common way.
> (30–33)

Whereas the opening speech presented Volpone as eloquent spokesman for mankind's universal adoration of riches, the turn here distinguishes him from (and places him above) the world at large, as Barabas had set off his "means of traffic from the vulgar trade," and as Richard had so emphatically opposed himself alone against a peaceful England. But again, in the speeches that follow from both Volpone and Mosca, we hear first about the "common way" rather than about Volpone's cunning; again the focus moves outward in a satirical list of all those base means of grubbing for wealth that Volpone himself disdains. Only after this broad and biting survey do we learn what constitutes Volpone's uniquely "cunning purchase"—learn, that is, how his knavish pretense of being rich, heirless, and at death's door makes all men "observe" him and ply him with gifts:

> All which I suffer, playing with their hopes,
> And am content to coin 'em into profit,
> And look upon their kindness, and take more,
> And look on that; still bearing them in hand,
> Letting the cherry knock against their lips,
> And draw it by their mouths, and back again.
> (85–90)

Thus Volpone cockers up his genius and prepares us to enjoy his knavery with him. But that so much of our early attention has been directed out at the greedy world on which the fox preys characterizes an essential feature of this play. Whereas Richard and Barabas seized all our interest at once and dominated it throughout, Jonson's fools claim a large share of it for themselves. That the objects of our derision should loom large is appropriate to satiric comedy, of course. But the satiric bias of this opening dialogue has partially diverted our first impressions away from the two knaves even while they are alone onstage. And the show performed by Volpone's odd attendants, which follows immediately, keeps the opening focus on universal folly rather than particular knavery: "Fools, they are the only nation" (1.2.66).

This is not to say that we are not interested as well in the intriguing pair who describe the way of the world so vividly for us, and we can both share their scorn for the "common way" and smile with Volpone at the apparent ease with which he teases the hopes of his would-be heirs, "letting the cherry knock against their lips." But from their first exchange, we are made to watch the relationship between the magnifico and his man "with considerate eyes." Such scrutiny is anathema to a knave, according to Richard, and it checks our full engagement with these two even when we enjoy their cunning purchase in something like their own spirit. The very fact that we watch them interact before the knave-hero presents himself directly to us distinguishes the opening of this play from either *Richard III* or *The Jew of Malta*. And what piques our interest in the two knaves here is the *way* they interact. To what extent is Mosca playing on, as well as to, Volpone? And to what extent is Volpone aware of the play between them? We notice that Mosca, after his somewhat curt interruption of the opening rhapsody, redirects his master's disdain of the common way through fulsome and obviously self-serving praise of Volpone's own munificence:

> *Mosca*: But, your sweet nature doth abhor these courses.
> . . . . .
> *Volp*: Right, Mosca, I do loathe it.
> . . . . .
> *Mosca*: You know the use of riches, and dare give, now,
>   From that bright heap, to me, your poor observer,
>   Or to your dwarf, or your hermaphrodite,
>   Your eunuch, or what other household trifle
>   Your pleasure allows maintenance—
> *Volp*:   Hold thee, Mosca,
>   [*Gives him money*]
>   Take, of my hand; thou strik'st on truth in all,
>   And they are envious term thee parasite.
> (48–68)

Just how are we to understand this "affectionate" exchange? Clearly Mosca gets what he wants from it; but is such subservient truckling the full extent of his art, or does his control over his nominal master have larger aims? And is Volpone simply basking in the sweet oil of this flattery? Is his interruption of it ("Hold thee Mosca, / Take, of my hand") the overflowing climax toward which Mosca's warm praise has worked him or a knowing signal that Mosca has sufficiently made his point and his pitch? What edge, if any, does he give to his reminder that the customary term for his "beloved Mosca's" place among the "household trifles" is "parasite"?[3]

Confirmed answers to some of these questions—notably those concerning Mosca's aims—can only depend on much later developments. The striking fact for an audience taking its bearings on these knaves is that our interest in them continues to involve such questions, since neither of them offers us any confidential answers for the time being. Richard presents "himself alone" so fully that we know precisely what he means when he calls Buckingham "my other self, my counsel's consistory, / My oracle, my prophet, my dear cousin," and we can therefore smile ironically with him as he gives himself over "as a child" to follow Buckingham's direction (2.2.151–53). And though Barabas sometimes tricks us, he never leaves us long in doubt about his true feelings toward his "trusty Ithamore":

> Thus every villain ambles after wealth,
> Although he ne'er be richer than in hope.
> But hush 't.
> (3.4.50–52)

But where their own relationship is concerned, neither Volpone nor Mosca gives us any such secret tips to "hush" until very near the end. Volpone tells us nothing to belie his apparently absolute trust in his parasite and though we see that such trust must be misplaced, we don't know Mosca's own mind. And so we watch these two observantly, with a kind of curiosity and expectancy that formed no part of our interest in Richard's knavery or in Barabas's.

The result is a virtual double focus for us when Volpone and Mosca go to work on the fools. While we enjoy their game, we keep an eye on what promises to be an equally interesting match between the knaves themselves. And what we see of Volpone through the first four acts exposes the vulnerabilities that will ultimately make that match fatal to him, not the least of which is his apparent unawareness that any such challenge from Mosca is in the offing. To the extent that we see him so exposed, of course, we maintain our elevation over him and our comic detachment from him and his professed cunning.

As he sets the scene for the fools' first entrance, for example, Volpone displays both his knavish control and the weakness that threatens it:

> Fetch me my gown,
> My furs, and night-caps; say my couch is changing.
> . . . . . .
> Now, now, my clients
> Begin their visitation! Vulture, kite,
> Raven, and gorcrow, all my birds of prey,
> That think me turning carcass, now they come.
> I am not for 'em yet.
> (1.2.84–91)

Here he is very much "our" knave, savoring his scheme and sharing his backstage preparations with us. But something else emerges when Mosca reports that the large piece of plate brought as an offering by the hopeful Voltore has Volpone's "name inscribed, / And arms engraven":

> *Volp*:   Good! and not a fox
>   Stretched on the earth, with fine delusive sleights
>   Mocking a gaping crow? ha, Mosca!
> *Mosca*:   Sharp, sir.
> (92–96)

It is perfectly in keeping that the fox, as he relishes the emblem of his knavery, should delight in his own triumphant wit. We were never so much in tune with Richard as when he first did so ("Was ever woman in this humor won?"). But Jonson adds a twist to his knave's witty mockery through the tell-tale need for appreciation exposed in its final appeal ("ha, Mosca!") and through Mosca's obediently flattering response to the cue. That revealed need alters the color of Volpone's professed glory in his own cunning somewhat. It could, with more emphasis, mark the difference between the "fine delusive sleights" of a knavish *eiron* and the self-delusive flights of a boasting *alazon*. The emphasis here is on Volpone's knavery, not his folly. But Mosca, as he laughs with Volpone at the fools whose assumption that "there's nought impossible" makes them such easy game, is also evidently probing to see how far Volpone's own hold on reality may be weakened by self-infatuation or thirst for flattery:

> *Volp*: Dispatch, dispatch. I long to have possession
>   Of my new present.
> *Mosca*:   That, and thousands more,
>   I hope to see you lord of.
> *Volp*:   Thanks, kind Mosca.
> *Mosca*: And that, when I am lost in blended dust,
>   And hundreds such as I am, in succession —
> *Volp*: Nay, that were too much, Mosca.
> *Mosca*:   You shall live
>   Still to delude these harpies.
> *Volp*:   Loving Mosca!
>   'Tis well.
> (116–23)

How far might "loving Mosca" delude Volpone along with "these harpies"? We will watch to see. Meanwhile, through such an exchange, the relationship between master and man holds its share of our speculative attention along with the game they will now play so adroitly with their victims.

The remainder of act 1 is given over to the successive rounds of that game, in which Voltore, Corbaccio, and Corvino are fed full of hope and bilked of their gifts. The action moves swiftly now, and it consistently directs our laughter at the dupes whose greedy folly amuses us as it does the artful knaves. The respective roles these two play, however, allow Mosca to upstage his master throughout their show. Volpone, of course, remains the clever fox who lures the foolish birds to him and who is, though prostrate, elevated above them in his mockery. He had ordered Mosca about in the backstage preparations, and this mastery may extend to the show itself insofar as Mosca's agile art serves

Volpone's pleasure as well as ours. But Volpone does not, and cannot, simply laugh with us. Though he manages one or two ironic thrusts of his own at Voltore ("You give, sir, what you can" [1.3.21]), his role subsides into that of a near-carcass on display, a decaying prop for Mosca's brisk act. Once the show begins, in fact, it is Mosca who gives Volpone hurried directions between scenes: "Keep you still, sir;" "Betake you to your silence, and your sleep"; "Close to your couch again" (1.3.79; 1.4.1, 160). And the directions spell out the constraints of Volpone's part in "his" play. As he himself describes his three-year run in it, in fact, it all sounds rather more like work than like play:

> Now, my feigned cough, my phthisic, and my gout,
> My apoplexy, palsy, and catarrhs,
> Help, with your forcèd functions, this my posture,
> Wherein, this three year, I have milked their hopes.
> (1.2.124–27)

In that posture he endures abuse that inevitably makes him partly the target of our laughter along with the eager "heir" who helps Mosca bombard his ear with insults:

Corvino: Art sure he does not hear us?
Mosca: Sure, sir? why, look you, credit your own sense.
  [*Shouts in Volpone's ear.*] The pox approach and add
    to your diseases,
  If it would send you hence the sooner, sir,
  For, your incontinence, it hath deserved it
  Throughly and throughly, and the plague to boot.
  You may come near, sir—Would you would once close
  Those filthy eyes of yours that flow with slime
  Like two frog-pits, and those same hanging cheeks,
  Covered with hide instead of skin—Nay, help, sir—
  That look like frozen dish-clouts set on end.
Corv: Or, like an old smoked wall, on which the rain
  Ran down in streaks.
Mosca: Excellent, sir, speak out.
  You may be louder yet; a culverin
  Dischargèd in his ear would hardly bore it.
Corv: His nose is like a common sewer, still running.

> *Mosca*: 'Tis good! And what his mouth?
> *Corv*:   A very draught.[4]
> (1.5.50–66)

When Mosca uses him so roughly, we may wonder if Volpone, his eyes clogged with makeup ointment, sees the show quite as we do. "Does he not perceive us?" asks Corvino; "No more than a blind harper," answers the mocking Mosca (38–39). Is the mock double-edged, cutting at Volpone as well as the anxious fool? Echoes through this scene that align Mosca's manipulation of the dupes with his handling of Volpone might prompt us to suspect as much. Just as he had flattered Volpone, so he flatters them. Each thinks, as Volpone does, that Mosca labors for him alone (1.4.119–23). Mosca instructs the would-be heirs how to act, as he directs Volpone himself here. And Volpone's voluptuous delight in Mosca's art finds its somewhat paler twin in Corvino's warm appreciation. Indeed, some of Mosca's exchanges with Volpone and with his other "masters" seem just of a kind:

> *Volp*: O, but thy working, and thy placing it!
>   I cannot hold; good rascal, let me kiss thee.
>   I never knew thee in so rare a humor.
> *Mosca*: Alas, sir, I but do as I am taught;
>   Follow your grave instructions; give 'em words;
>   Pour oil into their ears, and send them hence.
> *Volp*: 'Tis true, 'tis true.
> (1.4.136–42)

> *Mosca*:   Is not all here yours?
>   Am not I here, whom you have made? Your creature?
>   That owe my being to you?
> *Corvino*:   Grateful Mosca!
>   Thou art my friend, my fellow, my companion,
>   My partner, and shalt share in all my fortunes.
> (1.5.77–81)

There is, of course, a crucial difference. When Mosca pours oil into the dupes' ears, we know the immediate scheme and how it works. Where Volpone is concerned, we have no way of knowing so surely. Our view of this pair is speculative and continues so when Mosca dangles the bright image of Celia before Volpone to close out the first act, much as Volpone had said toward the beginning of it that he dangled the cherry of his wealth before the fools' greedy lips. Volpone was then openly explaining his knavish plot to us. But if Mosca has anything more in mind than his master's obvious pleasure in the very thought of Celia, he characteristically keeps his own counsel about it.

To say that we are given a more detached view of Volpone through the first movement of his play than we were of either Richard or Barabas does not at all imply that we are not interested in him. He may in fact be a more substantially complex and interesting character, as such, than either of those villainous knaves. But the human needs and weaknesses that may make him so handicap his knavery and the comic exposure of them prevents our full engagement in it. If the three middle acts of the play, revolving around his abortive suit of the prim Celia, intensify our interest in Volpone, they also heighten our perspective on his failings as a knave and increase our sense of his paradoxical dependence on his parasite.

Even the expansive performance as Scoto of Mantua, in which Volpone's acting skills might show to most advantage, is staged in a way that enforces our detached and amused observation rather than our appreciative participation in the performer's game. When a knave's show is framed by his own "induction" and "epilogue" for our ears only and conducted with ironic asides (the handling of the fools in act 1 exemplifies this common model, though with a pair of knaves), his controlling line of communication with the audience is kept fully open. But here the frame, complete with asides, is provided by the onstage audience of Peregrine and Sir Politic Wouldbe. Our interest in Volpone's performance is deflected out to their respectively witty and foolish responses to it. And the very skill of Volpone's realistically detailed portrayal of Scoto allows us to include our proper disdain of such actual charlatans in our satirical amusement at Sir Pol's credulity. Nothing is done through Scoto's long descent from eight crowns to sixpence that plays significantly on our awareness of the fox in mountebank's clothing. Only when Celia throws her handkerchief down from the window does Volpone's pursuit of her emerge through the apparently gratuitous verismo of his Scoto. And that pursuit culminates quickly in what Mosca later calls the unhappy "epilogue" to his master's show, as the enraged Corvino suddenly enters and pummels the offending mountebank and his followers off the stage. Right up to its catastrophe, therefore, Volpone's extended solo (for once Mosca's role shrinks to that of supernumerary) is presented in a way that submerges his knavish scheme and minimizes our engagement in it.

If we are distanced from Volpone through this long scene, the short one that follows gives us a more revealing close-up of him than any we have seen thus far. However comically demeaning his hasty exit under Corvino's jealous fire might have seemed, Volpone surely looks worse to us in this brief "backstage" exposure than he did "onstage" as Scoto. Perhaps we can credit him with some self-conscious irony when he hyperbolizes his plight as a woebegone lover in the most derivative Petrarchan mode:

> But angry Cupid, bolting from her eyes,
> Hath shot himself into me like a flame;
> Where, now, he flings about his burning heat,
> As in a furnace an ambitious fire
> Whose vent is stopped.

Nonetheless, the condition of being rendered helpless by one's own driving needs ought to characterize the knave's easiest victims rather than the master knave himself:

> The fight is all within me.
> I cannot live except thou help me, Mosca;
> My liver melts, and I, without the hope
> Of some soft air from her refreshing breath,
> Am but a heap of cinders.
> (2.4.3–11)

Indeed, there is little except Volpone's fervor to distinguish the exchange that follows from Mosca's earlier handling of the would-be heirs:

> *Mosca*: But I'm bound in conscience,
>   No less than duty, to effect my best
>   To your release of torment, and I will, sir.
> *Volp*: Dear Mosca, shall I hope?
> *Mosca*: Sir, more than dear,
>   I will not bid you to despair of aught

> Within a human compass.
> *Volp*:   O, there spoke
>   My better angel. Mosca, take my keys,
>   Gold, plate, and jewels, all's at thy devotion;
>   Employ them how thou wilt; nay, coin me too,
>   So thou in this but crown my longings—Mosca?
> *Mosca*: Use but your patience.
>   (15–25)

On his side, Mosca bespeaks "conscience" and "duty" in the best manner of knavish hypocrisy while Volpone swallows the fat bait of hope that covers all hooks for folly (cf. 1.4.134–35). But our growing sense that the master may be playing fool to his servant is no more damaging to Volpone's image as an artful knave than is his evident insecurity about that image and his urgent need to have it bolstered by flattery, both of which surface when he reviews his performance as Scoto:

> *Volp*: Is not the color o' my beard and eyebrows
>   To make me known?
> *Mosca*:   No jot.
> *Volp*:   I did it well.
> *Mosca*: So well, would I could follow you in mine,
>   With half the happiness; and, yet, I would
>   Escape your epilogue.
> *Volp*:   But were they gulled
>   With a belief that I was Scoto?
> *Mosca*:   Sir,
>   Scoto himself could hardly have distinguished!
>   I have not time to flatter you now; we'll part,
>   And as I prosper, so applaud my art.
>   (30–38)

We may at times look into other knaves with considerate eyes in ways that detach us from them, but what other knave exposes quite this same anxiety about his own craft? Volpone is by no means a would-be knave in the same sense that the foolish knight whom he has just deceived so completely is a would-be politician. He was, after all, superb as Scoto. But the fact that he worries thus at his knavery distinguishes him from those cavalier knaves who gleefully share their fun with us. It is this anxiety, in fact, that ultimately proves fatal to him. And it exposes him here not only to our critical observation but to the pointed barb with which the hitherto unctuous Mosca cuts his perfunctory praise short: "I have not time to flatter you now."[5]

Volpone is left, then, to nurse his hopes. While he is in that expectant posture, a hilarious scene subjects him to the torture of Lady Wouldbe's eternal tongue and our consequent laughter. Far from controlling this voluble fool, he lies as helpless under her verbal barrage as Sir Pol will be under his tortoise shell.[6] Once again the master knave is reduced to total dependence on his parasite, who rescues him with a "quick fiction" (3.5.25). But when Mosca has finally set the seduction scene, it is, of course, Volpone's turn to act it with his more-than-coy mistress.

If Celia had the dramatic power to evoke strong sympathy, our outrage at Volpone's assault on her might rival Bonario's and turn our amused interest in him toward revulsion. But several touches in this scene—the utter incongruity between the warm imagination with which he woos her ("Whilst we, in changèd shapes, act Ovid's tales") and the cold clichés with which she resists him, the sudden leap from his sickbed with which he begins his suit and the melodramatic leap from the closet with which Bonario ends it—can make it more comic than threatening. If so, the comedy turns (as it has from Corvino's drubbing through Lady Wouldbe's torrent of babble) against Volpone. But in any case, we see a double defeat for Volpone's cunning knavery, a double deflation of his foxy self-image that leaves him "unmasked, unspirited, undone" (3.7.278). First of all, his art fails him. Celia is, of course, impervious to all the craft of his gilded tongue. If this failure seems more a matter of her cold chastity than his flawed art, we might recall Richard's stunning success in an even less likely suit. Here, however, it is not the cunning fox but the "libidinous swine" (267) who is lunging at his victim when Bonario bursts onstage to thwart him. The final resort to brute force is a sorry comedown for the would-be seducer. He begins by presenting himself as the irresistible artist who "attracted / The eyes and ears of all the ladies" at the court of "the great Valois" and sinks to what Bonario so flatly labels him—a "foul ravisher" (267). The knave's defeat is thus compounded. Forced to abandon the art through which he might win us as well as his victim, he is nonetheless thwarted in his blunt assault.

The fiasco leaves Volpone to finish out act 3 at his most comically abject. Literally at his wit's end ("What shall we do?" [3.8.11]), he can only pray for Mosca's success as the parasite tries to pick up the shattered pieces of their plot. Nor does act 4 allow Volpone to regain any command over the play or our view of it. What Mosca will refer to as "our masterpiece" (5.2.13), the marvelous trial scene in which the skillfully orchestrated fools transform Bonario and Celia from accusers into defendants, is in fact the parasite's own show. Volpone's only part in it—his single brief appearance in the entire fourth act—is to be carried onstage and then back off again as a speechless, cadaverous invalid (4.6.20–57). It is from this low ebb that he tries to restore himself in his own eyes and in ours as the master knave when the final act opens.

But before looking at Volpone's fatal attempt to revive himself by playing dead, something must be said about our relationship with Mosca to this point in the play. In several ways, the "fly" may seem a more foxy knave than his master. Volpone waits in anxious hope while Mosca artfully fetches Celia to his lair, and is left in even more anxious prayer while Mosca repairs the ruins of that encounter. In act 1, and again even more impressively in act 4, Mosca manipulates the fools with agile grace while Volpone plays his single supine role. And we have seen Mosca evidently manipulate his praise-thirsty master as well. Why, then, does the parasite not simply steal the spotlight from Volpone and become "our" knave? Why, that is, do we not see the show Mosca so largely controls from his point of view? For reasons, as I have suggested, that further distinguish Mosca from his overexposed master. Whereas we see into Volpone's weaknesses too clearly to have confidence in his knavery, Mosca doesn't take us into his knavish confidence at all, or not until the play is almost over. Through the first two acts, though we may suppose that he has designs for himself as well as for Volpone, Mosca has no soliloquy and speaks no asides for our ears only. We may enjoy his fun with the fools in something like his own spirit, but he never shares that spirit openly with us in Richard's knavish manner. "And as I prosper, so applaud my art": we may do so, but this closing line in act 2, scene 4, is addressed to Volpone, not to us, and in a context that provokes our speculative interest in Mosca's handling of his master more than it involves us in his game with their dupes.

When, therefore, Mosca finally appears alone onstage to open act 3 by telling us about himself and his craft, we might expect to learn at last how he sees his role in the play he's been staging, and what he plans to do with it; but if he has a plot, he tells us nothing of it. His vaunting speech differs markedly in this respect from the normal mode of knavish confidentiality. It might seem to be of a kind with Richard's arch survey of his villainous skills in *3 Henry VI*, and surely each of these knaves takes pride in similar arts:

> *Richard*: I can add colors to the chameleon,
>   Change shapes with Proteus for advantages.
> (3.2.191–92)

> *Mosca*: But your fine, elegant rascal . . . can rise
>   And stoop, almost together, like an arrow;
>   · · · · ·
>   And change a visor swifter than a thought.
> (3.1.23–29)

But even these brief excerpts indicate the crucial difference that emerges so emphatically through the soliloquies as they are delivered entire. Richard focuses insistently on what *he* can do, and the singular "I" rings through virtually every line as he displays himself alone for our fascination. Though Mosca begins by preening himself in something like Richard's sportive way ("I fear I shall begin to grow in love / With my dear self and my most prosp'rous parts"), his self-exhibition takes an early turn into general satirical discourse:

>   O! your parasite
> Is a most precious thing, dropped from above,
> Not bred 'mongst clods and clodpolls, here on earth.
>   · · · · ·

> Almost
> All the wise world is little else in nature
> But parasites or sub-parasites.
> (3.1.7–13)

As in the speeches on universal greed with which the play opened, we focus out toward a world crawling with parasites, and here, as there, the knave's own distinction is defined first and at some length by the negative foil of the baser sort who pass in satirical review ("And yet, / I mean not those that have your bare town-art"). Even when Mosca turns in conclusion to the finer art that elevates him above these "sub-parasites," he leaves the portrait objectified in its general kind: "*Such* sparks / Are the true parasites, others but their zanies" (13–33). Such a speech, which pointedly holds the fawning behavior it describes (in both its lower and higher forms) up for our satiric inspection, is scarcely designed to engage us with the speaker as Richard's does.[7] Nor does Mosca take us into his scheme in Richard's customary knavish way ("Plots have I laid"). We know nothing more of his larger aims or of his real attitude toward Volpone than we did before this "confidential" address. In fact, the scenes that immediately follow may leave the uninformed audience wondering why Mosca should hide Bonario in Volpone's chambers, where he can overhear and interrupt the assault on Celia. In any case, the almost predictably catastrophic result of this attempt to juggle simultaneously a Bonario plot with a Celia plot falls on Mosca's swollen head ("success hath made me wanton") as well as on his master's, turning the knavish vaunt with which he opened this act into an overreacher's boast. The Mosca who picks his way out of the debris of the third act is not "our" knave, and though we must admire his dazzling recovery in act 4, the whole play has been designed to make us watch his moves rather than to see things his way. We don't even know yet what his way really is.

While Mosca thus continues to keep his own counsel, Volpone opens act 5 by exposing himself still more nakedly to our considerate eyes. The scene's structure is of a kind that might invite our fullest participation with the two knaves as they exult in their success, plan their next move, and then carry it off to their own delight and the fools' discomfiture. Summarized thus, it sounds like the very model of engaging knavery. But the curious soliloquy with which Volpone introduces this sequence lends an entirely different dimension to its sport.

That he is trying to rally himself after the admitted terrors he suffered under public gaze in the Scrutineo may put us in mind of Richard on the eve of Bosworth: "Give me a bowl of lusty wine to fright / This humor from my heart" (5.1.11–12). What makes Volpone unique among knaves, however, is the way in which he consciously calls upon his craft to settle his nerves and restore his self-esteem:

> Well, I must be merry
> And shake it off. A many of these fears
> Would put me into some villainous disease
> Should they come thick upon me. I'll prevent 'em.
> . . . . . .
> Any device, now, of rare, ingenious knavery
> That would possess me with a violent laughter,
> Would make me up again.
> (7–16)

Mirth, then, is not the spontaneous and infectious spirit that informs the playful knave's mischief. It is, rather, a determined act of will, a therapy sought, like the wine, "to fright / This humor from" his heart. We see what follows, therefore, not simply as Volpone's fun, but as his prescribed *use* of fun to quell the dread within. As a general rule, knavery flourishes most winningly for us as it approaches Puck's pure play—as it seems exempt, that is, from the needs and anxieties that both compel and limit us as foolish mortals. Invulnerable in its carefree enjoyment of the game itself (as we can be, for the nonce, as an audience in a theater), knavery plays on others' vulnerabilities: "Yet, I glory / More in the *cunning purchase* of my wealth / Than in the glad possession." But Volpone's very play now becomes an acknowledged matter of need and thus itself a symptom of vulnerability: "I *must* be merry" (7).[8]

In the triumphant review of their "masterpiece" that follows, we see Mosca's evident awareness of this vulnerability as he repeatedly probes beneath the visor of knavish high spirits that Volpone now tries to keep securely in place:

> *Mosca*: You are not taken with it enough, methinks?
> *Volp*: O, more than if I had enjoyed the wench.
>   The pleasure of all womankind's not like it.
> *Mosca*: Why, now you speak, sir!
>   . . . . .
> *Volp*:   I had much ado
>   To forbear laughing.
> *Mosca*:   'T seemed to me you sweat, sir.
> *Volp*: In troth, I did a little.
> *Mosca*:   But confess, sir;
>   Were you not daunted?
> *Volp*:   In good faith, I was
>   A little in a mist, but not dejected;
>   Never but still myself.
> *Mosca*:   I think it, sir.
>   (5.2.9–41)

Such exchanges, with the added light of the soliloquy that precedes them, focus our attention even more sharply than before on the hidden interplay between the knaves. As Volpone outlines his nervously exuberant plot to vex the gulls by naming Mosca his "actual" heir while he plays dead, we notice that Mosca, who must now sense his advantage, indulges in such palpable hits as his reminder of that telltale sweat (98). But Volpone is not to be reminded. His plan for escaping (he would call it "conquering") unpleasant thoughts about himself is working all too well. Even Mosca is startled into an incredulous "Who?" by his master's sudden leap out of context and onto a new plane of self-comforting delusion with "I think she [Celia] loves me," though the agile parasite recovers quickly enough to feather this dream-cloud with flattery (106–7).[9]

At this point Volpone retires behind a screen and asks us to share his pleasure in the performance of what he supposes is his own play, in which Mosca as the surprised "heir" taunts the fools who have so amply padded "his" fortune:

Volp: Now they begin to flutter;
They never think of me. Look, see, see, see!
How their swift eyes run over the long deed
Unto the name.
. . . . .
                              Now their hopes
Are at the gasp.
. . . . .
Rare, Mosca! How his villainy becomes him!

As choral cheerleader, Volpone may accurately express our
response to the action he is watching. But he can't guide or share
our full response, since that includes our view of him and of the
extent to which he has just exposed himself as a would-be
knave.[10] We are bound to feel that his position is precariously
close to that of Voltore, who mistakenly supposes, as he sees
Mosca turn the other gulls away, that "he doth delude all these
for me" (62). We still don't know, however, just where Mosca
places Volpone in his own view. And so, when the dejected
"heirs" have all been purged, we watch the knaves' final embrace
with heightened expectancy, sharing neither the master's ecstasy
nor the parasite's schemes and sensing that the two must now
collide at any moment (102 ff.).

That collision course is finally revealed openly when the pair
next appears newly costumed—Volpone disguised as a commendatore to harry the vexed fools through the streets and Mosca
now dressed bravely in his master's own robes as a "clarissimo."
The ominous overtones of Mosca's knavish speech now sleep
soundly in Volpone's foolish ear:

Mosca: But what am I?
Volp: 'Fore heav'n, a brave *clarissimo,* thou becom'st it!
    Pity thou wert not born one.
Mosca: If I hold
    My made one, 'twill be well.
(5.5.2–5)

And as Volpone leaves, now fully "possessed" (as he had sought
to be) by his new "device" (5.1.14–15), Mosca at last unveils for us

his darker purpose against the master whom he now patroniz-
ingly calls "*my* fox":

> My fox
> Is out on his hole, and ere he shall re-enter,
> I'll make him languish in his borrowed case,
> Except he come to composition with me.
> . . . . .
>
> So, now I have the keys and am possessed.
> Since he will needs be dead afore his time,
> I'll bury him, or gain by him. I'm his heir,
> And so will keep me, till he share at least.
> To cozen him of all were but a cheat
> Well placed; no man would cònstrue it a sin.
> Let his sport pay for 't. This is called the fox-trap.
> (6–18)

"Possessed" thus in a much more advantageous sense than
Volpone, Mosca acidly assesses the cost of sport that is driven by
compulsive need and names the play, "the fox-trap," over which
he should now have complete control.

At this stage, it is too late for the parasite whom we have
watched with a suspicious eye for so long to enlist us as his
confidants in a way that will make us enjoy the end of the show
with him. He confirms our accurate suspicions, rather—confirms
us as proper "understanders"—and we continue to look on from
our secure perspective as such. In any event, we see comparatively
little of Mosca after his open revelation. Once we know for sure
about the parasite's scheme against him, the focus is on Volpone,
whom we can now watch for the first time in the full ironic light
of this awareness. Seen thus, Volpone's biting mockery of the
fleeced fools inevitably backfires upon him:

> *Volp*:   In good faith, sir,
> I'm heartily grieved a beard of your grave length
> Should be so over-reached. I never brooked
> That parasite's hair; methought his nose should cozen.
> There still was somewhat in his look did promise
> The bane of a *clarissimo*.
> (5.8.4–9)

Exactly! And the angry epithet that Voltore flings at this pesky commendatore, "Mistaking knave!" now fits Volpone like a glove (5.7.21).

When the smitten Voltore is provoked into a ruinous public confession, therefore, our perspective on Volpone's first recognition of his mistake, "I'm caught / I' mine own noose," is broadly comic (5.10.13–14). It is the comedy of Volpone's inevitable collapse that we have been prepared to enjoy from our vantage point all along. Though he catches sight of the noose settling around him, he himself never rises to a full view of the motives that prompted him into its reach. It is more flattering to his coveted knavish image of himself to blame the "mere wantonness" of his fatal "fine conceits" than to recall the anxiety that actually impelled them (act 5, scene 11). Even his last frantic effort to unscramble his error under the very eyes of public officialdom (as Mosca had managed to do in the preceding act) is built on the futile hope that the parasite is still *his* knave (5.11.18). We know better, of course, and Volpone's final juggling of the ever-pliable fools looks all the more ludicrously absurd under the shadow of his impending confrontation with the truth. There is no surprise for us—only the tense expectancy of the shock in store for Volpone—when the two knaves whose unstable alliance has caught our attention from the beginning now meet head-on, and Mosca's arrogant hostility is at last revealed even to his master's reluctant eyes. Since the parasite's firm counterplot, bolstered by every advantage (including the support of the obliging avocatori), can only be exploded by the self-destructive revelation toward which Volpone's desperate asides build through this sequence, the catastrophe for which Jonson apologized in his prefatory letter seems at this point in perfect keeping with the whole play's comic "promise" (Epistle, 104–6). It is fitting that the master and his overreaching parasite should be "mulcted" and that the "cunning" knave whose weaknesses have been comically exposed throughout should fall in his own trap along with his foolish victims.

If what has been said thus far stresses our view of Volpone's vulnerability and understates our frequent enjoyment of his wit, the emphasis on the former is intended to clarify our distinctive relationship with this complex knave. As we move from speculation to a more certain advantage in awareness over him, our consequent detachment and elevation make this play more a comic study of knavery for us than an abandoned frolic with it. Act 5, in particular, has played to our superior vantage point.

And yet, at the very end, Volpone manages to surprise us after all, and not only with the nobility of his final self-assertion. There is a new assurance in his brief speech putting knaves and fools in their respective places, certainly; its very brevity and directness save it from swelling into one more inflated boast from the fox who has always fed too hungrily on flattery and self-praise. What may tell even more favorably for us in this comedy, however, is Volpone's cavalier demeanor through the harsh aftermath of his confession. It is not just the hero's fall, of course, but the cruel and unusual punishment inflicted upon him by the suddenly righteous avocatori that Jonson correctly supposed might provoke some critical questions about his conclusion. The judgment's severity threatens the ending of the comedy we have been enjoying.[11] But morality does not swamp humor entirely even here. What may be surprising, given the prayer and the palsy to which his fears of exposure have heretofore reduced him, is that Volpone alone maintains the comic spirit for us through this otherwise solemn conclusion and thus keeps stern judgment from closing down our fun too oppressively. As the avocatori sentence them and moralize over them, the fools (or those who can hear) fall into futile pleas and bitter shame. Mosca, all his wit and mockery spent, can only manage a vicious snarl at his erstwhile master. But when Volpone totally forsakes the fool's bait of "hope" in his confession, he also passes by the grim hook of "despair" (5.12.92–93). Safe from these snares of mortal folly, he can be a true knave at last, capable of greeting both Mosca's sentence and his own with sardonic wit. It is he who can thereby give his play its final comic title: "This is called mortifying of a fox" (125); he who thus earns the right to ask our jovial applause in the Epilogue. As he comes forward to do so, he decorously professes a performer's modesty by saying that he stands "doubtful" before us until we clap with approval. A doubtful stance has, in fact, too often subverted his knavery in our eyes earlier on. But not now. At the very end he earns the knavish laurel he had claimed from the beginning, and by jauntily facing up to the sober judges he makes good an earlier boast: "The fox fares . . . best when he is cursed" (5.3.119).

4

Vindice

THE INNOCENT VILLAIN

The Revenger's Tragedy treats us to a kaleidoscopic spectacle "of carnal, bloody, and unnatural acts, / Of accidental judgments, casual slaughters, / Of deaths put on by cunning and forced cause, / And . . . purposes mistook / Fall'n on th' inventors' heads" that might make the story Horatio promises to tell Fortinbras seem, by comparison, a round unvarnished tale.[1] Nor are we allowed to watch this play from the secure elevation of the blazing star that hovers so portentously over its conclusion, or with the sure vision of "that eternal eye / That sees through flesh and all" (1.3.66–67). Instead, we are involved more thoroughly in the sometimes vexed point of view of the intriguing hero, Vindice, than has been the case with any knave encountered here since Richard made us enjoy his first successes with him. But our experience with Vindice differs so sharply from that with Richard that the two best set one another off by the light of contrast. Richard's pure villainy was easy enough to place as such, though neither he nor we enjoy that villainy by the end of his play in the same spirit that enlivened its beginning. Vindice, less at ease than Richard with his own assumption of the knave's role, is also more difficult to label satisfactorily. The oxymoron he himself employs when he cries out that he and his brother "are made . . . innocent villains" may offer as fair a characterization of this revenger as we can make (1.3.167). If so, however, the meaning of the adjective changes through the course of the play, as does our perspective on Vindice. Through the first two acts we watch him prove too "innocent" (or naive) a villain to manage the world of knaves he has entered. In the second half of the play he becomes villain enough—and knave enough—to control that world and to make us appreciate his control of it with him, but he remains "innocent" in ways that distinguish him from the decadent "nest of dukes" he brings down. The conclusion allows us to evade such a complex and relative moral assessment, I believe; but if we make it nonetheless, our judgment would support the theatrical engagement with Vindice's knavery toward which his growing command of the action prompts us.[2]

If Vindice's progress from frustration to success finally stands in sharp contrast to Richard's loss of control, some telling differences between the clearer contours of Richard's world and the more tortuous ways of *The Revenger's Tragedy* are apparent from the very beginning. Like Richard, Vindice serves as the expository presenter of the play he opens for us, and like Richard, he sets himself off as antagonist to the world he describes as he introduces himself and the Duke's court to us. Vindice's antagonism has a radically different basis, of course. Whereas Richard brazenly sets his determined villainy against a world at peace, Vindice stands before us (with the skull of his late "betrothed lady") as the anguished victim of a villainous world. If the difference were a simple reversal of the conflict between virtue and villainy, however, offering us a Richmond-like hero in Richard's place, *The Revenger's Tragedy* would be a much less intriguing play than it is. Instead, Vindice's opening speech is disturbing in ways that Richard's mischievous mood never was. Both presenters command our initial view of their plays completely; but, paradoxically, the perturbed victim makes it less comfortable for us to share his view than the professed villain had.

The ease with which we began to enjoy Richard's knavery depended very much on the clarity with which he placed himself in a world of neatly balanced opposites ("And if King Edward be as true and just / As I am subtle, false, and treacherous"), on his own relish for his self-designated role as villain in that world, on the deft control he immediately asserted in that role, and on the playful wit with which he presented all of this to us. As we first see him, Vindice differs in every respect. His melancholic vision confounds the clear distinctions of Richard's easy antitheses in the twisted language of paradox, where apparent incompatibles mate in grotesque combinations. Instead of "false" villain versus "true" king, we have a "bastard *true*-begot in *evil*" and the "gray-hair'd adultery" and "palsy-lust" of his father the Duke, whose "marrowless age" somehow stuffs his "hollow bones with damn'd desires." The contradictions here do not complicate our view of the court by modifying its viciousness with a mixture of good. Rather, evil is compounded in a disturbing way when we hear that the bastard who embodies it is "true-begot" in it and more so when we hear that it prevails over nature in the "juiceless" duke's "spendthrift veins."[3] Such unpleasant paradoxes find their expression through wit, of course, and we must appreciate the wit that charges Vindice's opening lines if we are going to savor this play at all. This is not, however, the detached, mocking wit with which Richard first amused us. The exclamatory "O!" that regularly punctuates Vindice's outburst indicates how far he is from such easy, playful control as he assails the Duke and his court:

> O God! one
> That has scarce blood enough to live upon,
> And he to riot it like a son and heir?
> O the thought of that
> Turns my abused heartstrings into fret.
> (9–13)

The fact that the energy of Vindice's wit comes from fret, not sport, accounts for the bitter edge with which his ironies cut and makes his view an uncomfortable one to share. We have no reason, nor will we be given any, to question the validity of his view of the court and thus hold back from it, but it is no fun to see things thus. We sense how rankled Vindice's own vision has become not only in his conscious use of his former lady's skull to further activate his "fret," but in the turn his thoughts take as he does so. Since the Duke had poisoned her for refusing to submit to his lust, Vindice might focus on the pure virtue of his betrothed as a positive counterpart to detested villainy in something like Richard's manner of balancing black against white. Instead, the memory of her beauty drives him on in the paradoxical mode of disillusioned bitterness as he imagines its ironically sinful effect:

> 'Twas a face
> So far beyond the artificial shine
> Of any woman's bought complexion
> That the uprightest man (if such there be,
> That sin but seven times a day) broke custom
> And made up eight with looking after her.
> (20–25)

Outrage that rails at the "accursed palace" and sees even "the uprightest man" in terms of his sins is inspired, of course, by satire's cankered muse, not by a knave's puckish spirit.[4] In fact, no antic disposition whatsoever shows through the first thirty-eight lines of Vindice's exposition. If he continued in this Juvenalian vein alone, the revenger would find no place in our story. But the call to vengeance with which he ends his opening speech sounds another note: "Be merry, merry." Whether spoken as self-exhortation or as encouragement to the skull with which his revenge is so closely identified, these words signal a change in Vindice's tone that carries through the ensuing dialogue with his brother. He readily joins in the self-consciously witty repartee ("Thou play'st upon my meaning"; "I reach you") with which Hippolito spices the good news that Vindice may now pursue his vengeance by enlisting as pander to the Duke's insatiable son and heir, Lussurioso. And in deciding to seize this occasion, Vindice formally assumes the mantle that fits his emerging role as "merry" schemer:

> And therefore I'll put on that knave for once,
> And be a right man then, a man o'th' time;
> For to be honest is not to be i'th' world.
> Brother, I'll be that strange-composed fellow.
> (93–96)

The knavish game's afoot, then. But, partly because Vindice cannot simply change from Thersites into Puck, his pursuit of that game involves complications that distinguish him from other knaves. Richard, through all his roles, is what he is, and we can enjoy or despise him accordingly. Vindice is a more "strange-composed fellow." The fret that underlies his sport still chafes against it somewhat. He must, after all, "*put on* that knave" and the need to buoy himself up to it ("Be merry, merry") gives the role he assumes some of the manic frenzy that tainted Volpone's sport after we saw him rouse his palsied spirit with strong drink ("I *must* be merry" [*Volpone*, 5.1.7]). Given our immediate involvement in Vindice's tortured point of view, we are not afforded the kind of detachment from him here that made Volpone vulnerable to our superior awareness. But the bitterness that persists in Vindice makes our initial participation in the spirit of his "put on" knavery less than totally comfortable.

If the emotion seething inside Vindice at first gives his knavish gaiety a nervous strain unlike the freer élan with which Richard set out to play, this opening speech reveals that he nonetheless draws on an ultimate source of detachment that remained beyond Richard's ken. The mocking skulls in Clarence's dream helped to provide the larger ironic perspective within which Richard's adroit moves and ambitious game shrank to the spasms of a giddy fall (*Richard III*, 1.4.16–33). But Vindice shares the skull's grim joke from the very beginning. It provides, in fact, the call to mirth with which he turns from fret to sport:

> Be merry, merry;
> Advance thee, O thou terror to fat folks,
> To have their costly three-pil'd flesh worn off
> As bare as this—for banquets, ease, and laughter
> Can make great men, as greatness goes by clay,
> But wise men little are more great than they!
> (44–49)

Though Vindice scarcely fits the image of calm sagacity that wise men who smile at worldly greatness call to mind, he does live by the lesson of the skull in ways that distinguish him radically from the court world he opposes here, as well as from Richard and most other knaves. Since neither lust nor ambition are any part of his purpose, since he sees the mortal folly of both just as the skull's unblinking eyes do, the tense revenger is ultimately more securely detached in his knavery than that cool villain, Richard. Richard's head becomes uneasy as soon as it wears the crown he had coveted. The only pleasure that Vindice seeks lies in the success of his knavish vengeance itself. When it comes, then, success accordingly dissipates the fret that initially motivated his knavery; and when his boast of that success costs him his life, Vindice's lighthearted response suits his long familiarity with the "shell of death" that, as his "studies' ornament," had taught him to accept this inevitable sentence (1.1.15).

If Vindice's memento mori finally serves him well, it is scarcely an adequate tutor for the role he takes on with such eager confidence in the opening scene. To "put on that knave for once" proves a hazardous enterprise for a novice in a world of seasoned villains. We see that world without Vindice's mediation in the second scene, and the "trial" that we witness here does perfect justice to his opening description of the vicious court (that is the *only* "perfect justice" done at this trial, of course). Lussurioso later shows off the knowledge he "never learnt in schools" by declaring that "the world's divided into knaves and fools" (2.2.4–5). His cynical dismissal of moral distinctions suits this totally corrupt court well enough, but Lussurioso's "division" is rather too absolute to apply here. All of these villains are knavish enough to try to play one another for fools, and most prove to be foolish knaves in the process. None, in fact, truly represents the witty knavery to which Vindice now aspires, and the ways in which they fall short of it set off his own assumption of that role for us. In this first ensemble appearance, the Duke and Lussurioso make some attempt to cover their self-interest with a thin veil of moral verbiage, but neither enlivens his deceit for us with any mischievous wit. The Duchess's Youngest Son, on the other hand, as the defendant on trial for a brutal rape, is jaunty enough for any knave, but is apparently so perfectly acclimated to the depravity of his world that he feels no call to gloss it over with knavish guile at all:

> *2nd Judge*:   Confess, my lord,
>   What mov'd you to't
> *Youngest Son*:   Why, flesh and blood, my lord.
>   What should move men unto a woman else?
> (1.2.46–48)

His brothers, the magnificently named Ambitioso and Super-vacuo, promise him "a trick" to set him free in knavish asides here, and their bumbling scheme will later provide the dull foil for Vindice's first witty triumph. The only character whose stance in this second scene openly demands comparison with Vindice as we have seen him thus far, however, is Spurio, the Duke's bastard son. The comparison is worth special attention here, since it shows so clearly how the play differentiates our view of, and response to, characters whose actions might, in and of themselves, be considered virtually equivalent.

Like Vindice, who looked on with "abused heartstrings" as the ducal procession crossed the stage to open the play, Spurio stands apart from the wrangling court in this trial scene, and his venomous asides match Vindice's deadly hatred of what he sees:

> [I] hope he [the Youngest Son] shall die;
> And if a bastard's wish might stand in force,
> Would all the court were turn'd into a corse.
> (34–36)

And the soliloquy with which Spurio caps this scene both plans his revenge against the Duke, as Vindice's opening soliloquy had anticipated his, and shares Vindice's bent for lurid satire. The bastard's verbal portrait of the "whisp'ring and withdrawing hour" when he was begot (179–88) is just of a kind with Vindice's later set pieces on the "fulsome lust" that keeps the court busily "juggling of all sides" through the night (1.3.57–71; 2.1.195–230; 2.2.132–44). The two, then, could be made to appear as soul mates. Instead, the distinctions that emerge here and that become even more pronounced when their separate roads to vengeance meet at the Duke's fatal rendezvous in act 3, all promote Vindice's knavery as the focus of our engagement in the play.

For one thing, Vindice's growing command over our point of view can be partly measured by his ability to contain Spurio's revenge plot within his own. His opening speech has already provided the sinister frame within which the bastard performs in the trial scene, of course, and we will see later how the climax of Spurio's vengeance is made a feature in Vindice's own spectacular show. But it is not only a matter of the greater knave stealing the lesser's scenes for his own purposes. Spurio never exercises the knave's means of engaging us into his plot at all, even when he emerges from Vindice's frame to address us on his own account. As he meditates his way into a vindictive acceptance of the Duchess's adulterous advances, he is totally lacking in the knavish spirit of free play, totally possessed by a dour consciousness of himself as the very embodiment of the sin he hates:

> Duke, thou didst do me wrong, and by thy act
> Adultery is my nature.
> . . . . .
> Duke, on thy brow I'll draw my bastardy.
> For indeed a bastard by nature should make cuckolds,
> Because he is the son of a cuckold-maker.
> (177–203).

There is no playful wit whatsoever in his brand of verbal transformation. "Now, hate, begin; / I'll call foul incest but a venial sin" (169–70); that is not, for Spurio, a knavish joke, but a solemn declaration, a desperate resolve akin to Satan's "Evil, be thou my good." Spurio's own spoilsport conscience insists that we see his vengeance as an enactment of the vicious court's sin in its most representative form. There can be no question, therefore, of enjoying the bastard's scheme with him, since it proves almost as baleful to him as to his victim. By sharp contrast, neither Vindice nor anyone else worries a whit about the possible guilt attached to his violent revenge before the last moment of the play. Until then, neither this issue nor the concern it could provoke are openly raised to inhibit our enjoyment of Vindice's success in his own increasingly gleeful spirit. Vindice may not be the sort of knave with whom it is most easy to relax and enjoy the show, but in a world so full of possible competitors, everything is done to highlight his knavery as the focus through which we experience the action and to make it the only engaging sport at work in the play (or at play in the work).[5]

To emphasize the contrast between them, we see Vindice enter to present himself as "the child o'th' court" on the heels of Spurio's exit as "the son of a cuckold-maker" (1.3.4). Whereas the bastard was acknowledging a bitter truth, Vindice, far from actually identifying himself with the Duke's world, is preening himself in the "false" knave's role that will give him subversive access to it: "What, brother, am I far enough from my self?" Fret is evidently under sportive control now, and we can smile along with Hippolito at Vindice's mocking invocation to Impudence, the "goddess of the palace" (5-16). But the humor of Vindice's knavish debut will take a sharp turn that neither he nor we can foresee in this brash beginning.

As the saucy Piato, Vindice controls his introduction into Lussurioso's service with an apparently sure hand. Since he is not the serviceable bawd Lussurioso so quickly takes him for, we enjoy the deception and its comic ironies from Vindice's superior level of awareness. But just as Vindice, now fully warmed to his part, is boasting of his crafty art—"Make known the lady to me, and my brain / Shall swell with strange invention" (119-20)— Lussurioso unwittingly pulls the cord that exposes Vindice as no "wondrous knave" after all, as still bearing in his cheeks too much of the "scholar" that he had supposedly put off with his invocation to Impudence. For it proves to be Vindice's own sister Castiza, presumably left safely behind and out of mind when he entered the villainous court, upon whom Lussurioso now means to set him as a corrupting pander.

The effect of this sudden turn is complex. It is broadly comic at the expense of Vindice's punctured overconfidence, of course. As we watch him squirm through the rest of this scene, his discomfiture is the opposite of knavish control, and the ironies that give the situation its point for us now become daggers in his entrails:

> *Luss*:   That was her brother
>   That did prefer thee to us.
>   . . . . .
>   We may laugh at that simple age within him—
> *Vind*: Ha, ha, ha. . . .
>   . . . . .
>   A pure novice!
> (132-42)

There is no antic glee in *that* forced laugh, nor in Vindice's recognition that he and his brothers are in fact novices in Lussurioso's sordid game. As he struggles to keep up his part, the contrast with Richard at a parallel stage in his career is again telling. Richard, perfectly in control of his situation, had archly proclaimed himself "too childish-foolish for this world" (1.3.141). That is precisely what Vindice discovers himself to be here, for all the bitter disillusionment of his opening soliloquy and all the sophisticated cynicism of the knavish mask he now works so strenuously to keep in place. The point is reinforced when Lussurioso puts Vindice down as a mere "puny in the subtle mystery of a woman" for his expressed doubt that a mother could be so moved "by any gifts" as to "become a bawd to her own daughter" (148–55), and is acknowledged by Vindice himself in the soliloquy that closes the scene he had begun so impudently. Sport has reverted to fret:

> O,
> Now let me burst, I've eaten noble poison;
> We are made strange fellows, brother, innocent villains.
> (165–67)

But we are in no position to laugh at Vindice as a simple fool when he spoils his knavish debut by tripping over Lussurioso's nasty surprise. We watch him neither with the antagonism that made us enjoy Barabas's frustrations nor with the superior awareness that put Volpone in a vulnerably comic light for us. Though the sudden awkwardness of Vindice's situation turns the scene's humor against him, his shock is nonetheless ours as well. We have followed him into this snare, and if we can afford the amusement it inevitably provokes as he cannot, we still share his discovery that the court world is more perilously vicious than even his abused imagination had fathomed. A mixture of humor and horror, of amusement and amazement, is, of course, this play's special forte, but it is served to us in differing ways through the course of the action. Here we are amused *at* Vindice and horrified *with* him; later, the reverse may be true. The double effect here may show in subtler ripples that threatened Vindice's smooth sailing even earlier in the scene. Lussurioso, in the process of examining "Piato's" knavish credentials, had touched on the crucial question of his previous experience with "strange lust." Vindice would seem not only to rise to the occasion but to soar high over it with the hyperbolic vision of "fulsome lust" his satirist's wit conjures up:

Some father dreads not (gone to bed in wine) to slide
From the mother, and cling the daughter-in-law;
Some uncles are adulterous with their nieces,
Brothers with brothers' wives: O hour of incest!
Any kin now, next to the rim o'th' sister,
Is man's meat in these days; and in the morning,
When they are up and dress'd, and their mask on,
Who can perceive this, save that eternal eye
That sees through flesh and all?
(59–67)

That Lussurioso takes this Juvenalian effort so blandly in stride as simple "troth" ("But let this talk glide. . . . Now, sir, . . ." [72–75]) and therefore as routine evidence that "Piato" is "well experienc'd" in the ordinary affairs of "this luxurious day wherein we breathe" (109–10) has both effects of rather comically deflating Vindice's effusion and at the same time expanding our sense of the awesome depravity that can actually breathe normally in such a world. This complex response to Vindice and his plight breaks out in full force when Lussurioso reveals Castiza as the next intended victim on his lecherous list. And the series of successful failures and catastrophic successes that mark Vindice's knavish progress through act 2 continue to prompt both our amusement at him and the amazement we share along with him.[6]

The contorted postures Vindice now finds himself in as he sets out in two directions at once—testing the virtue of his mother and sister on the one hand and attacking the vice of the court on the other—might be suggested by Hippolito's stifled retort to Lussurioso's smug division of the world into knaves and fools: "Knave in your face, my lord—behind your back" (2.2.6). On the home front, Vindice is knave enough to deceive his own family, but the ironies of his deception keep twisting around to stab him in the back. Though he makes Lussurioso's game to some extent his own when he subdues "angry froth" with "policy" and carries out Piato's role as pander (1.3.172–82), that role precludes the knave's enjoyment of his own controlling wit, since it puts enjoyment and control at odds for him. When he "fails" to entice his sister, he receives a buffoon's box on the ear and rejoices at it (2.1.30–48). When he "succeeds" in corrupting his mother, he is driven to anguished asides that echo his equally unknavish discomfiture in the preceding scene with Lussurioso:

> *Gratiana*: O heavens! this overcomes me!
> *Vind (aside)*: Not, I hope, already?
> (2.1.103–4)

Once again he has confidently staged a scene ("I durst, almost for good, / Venture my lands in heaven upon their blood" [1.3.181–82]), only to have it turn suddenly against him.

Back at court, we watch Vindice drift further out of his depth in the vicious crosscurrents of intrigue. The reversals that baffle his attempts to direct events bring the first stage of his career as an "innocent villain" to a happier conclusion at the end of act 2 than he has any right to expect. Knowing of Spurio's intended assignation with the Duchess, Vindice sees the bastard approach with "two of his valiant bawds" and stands back to "observe his passage" (2.2.113–17). This stage situation might normally align Vindice as an informed onlooker with the audience and put him one up on the bastard. Instead, we hear what Vindice misses and know that he is operating on a misunderstanding of Spurio's "soft and wary" exit when he derails Lussurioso into an attempt to catch the bastard and his stepmother hard at it. The resulting blunder, in which the sword-wielding Lussurioso surprises the Duchess in bed with (*mirabile dictu!*) her own husband, proves to be one of Vindice's most successful failures:

> *Vind*: His vicious purpose to our sister's honor
>   Is cross'd *beyond our thought.*
> *Hipp*:   *You little dreamt*
>   His father slept here.
> *Vind*:   O, *'twas far beyond me.*
> (2.3.30–32; my italics)

As Vindice slinks stealthily out of harm's way for the nonce, everything indicates that knavish control of such a volatile situation is still far beyond him. He is, in his own words, too "shallow yet" to manipulate these events for his own ends and our amusement. Much of the latter has been triggered by reversals that catch him unaware. But if he is not yet our winning knave, he is never reduced to a hapless clown through these reversals. Neither the box on the ear nor the anguished asides make him the target of our derision in the way that Barabas sometimes was when he suffered the slings and arrows of outrageous fortune. We have experienced most of Vindice's surprises with him, and as an observer (if not director) of events he expresses our own view of things aptly enough both at home (where he cheers Castiza's virtue and winces at Gratiana's collapse) and at court. If he can't always share our laughter, we share his wonder at a world that consistently surpasses even his vast expectations of its depravity. And his reversals highlight that depravity at least as much as they expose the comic "innocence" of his maiden ventures in knavery.

Ambitioso and Supervacuo show us the difference between such innocence and foolish knavery that plays directly to our derisive laughter when they try to pick up the pieces of Vindice's fortunate fiasco and shape them to their own advantage. Everything is done to heighten the contrast between our complex experience of Vindice's reversals and our simple delight at theirs. We see their abortive plot to have Lussurioso executed entirely from our superior point of view. Having shared the old Duke's scorn for their all-too-obvious craft, "like scarlet hid in lawn, easily spied through," we know he will set Lussurioso free before they can deliver the "command of present death" for their "brother, the duke's son," to the officer; we can therefore see just how their plan will backfire—how their own younger brother, still in prison for rape and impatiently awaiting the "trick" by which they had promised his release, will fall neatly into Lussurioso's place as the victim of their palpable device (2.3.106; 3.3.2–3). In this clear light, both their boasting while they set up their plot and their curses when it collapses are broadly comic. The fraternal wrangling that makes these ninnies doubly ineffective as a team further reduces them to the level of burlesque and sharpens the contrast with Vindice, whose loyal brother lends him constant and sincere support ("You flow well, brother") that helps to steer our own appreciation. The clouds of "innocence" trailing over Vindice's knavish wit may have amused us at his expense, but not at all like the outright buffoonery with which Ambitioso and Supervacuo fill the interlude between his covert departure from the Duchess's busy bedroom and his return to the action five scenes later.[7]

Vindice's return is a triumphant one. No more will we see him overparted in his knave's role or watch the scenes he has entered burst out of his control. From this point on, Vindice directs the action with a masterful hand and enjoys it in the antic spirit of a true knave. The outburst with which he reenters announces the change: "O sweet, delectable, rare, happy, ravishing!" (3.5.1). This cry is far from those anguished exclamations that punctuated Vindice's opening soliloquy or the tormented asides through which he released the repeated frustrations of his earlier knavery. In fact, his ecstasy here, as he relishes the fatal scene he has contrived for the Duke, soars in terms that might normally forecast an overreacher's catastrophic plunge:

> O, 'tis able
> To make a man spring up, and knock his forehead
> Against yon silver ceiling.
> . . . . .
> I'm in a throng of happy apprehensions.
> (2-4, 30)

But in this astounding scene, not the least of our surprises is the finesse with which the hitherto hapless Vindice makes the old duke's tragedy entirely *his* play.

It is a production that rivals any of Richard's for knavish wit and surely outstrips any we have seen in shocking violence. Whereas Vindice had previously been victimized by the shocks that surprised us into laughter, he now controls both our amusement and our astonishment. His guiding hand manages every theatrical touch, including the makeup of Gloriana's poisoned skull and the lighting and special effects ("Back with the torch, brother; raise the perfumes" [139]), as the dry Duke's last assignation builds toward a climax he never dreamed of in his "damn'd desires." As audience, we are given a double treat. First we experience the full thrill of surprise as Vindice teasingly unveils his "bony lady" for Hippolito by way of preview; and after we are thus made privy to the scheme, we can enjoy

Vindice's ironies with him when he plays his pander's part and introduces this deadly concubine to the Duke: "Faith, my lord, . . . sh'as somewhat a grave look with her, but—" (132–35).[8]

The horror show that follows, in which the Duke is made spectator to his cuckolding before his tormentors finally stab him to death, is not mollified in the least with the sort of farcical antics that sometimes take the painful edge off knavish violence for us (as was the case, for example, with the murderous pranks of Barabas and Ithamore). On the contrary, the victim's pain is insisted upon as the very essence of revenge:

> Now I'll begin
> To stick thy soul with ulcers. I will make
> Thy spirit grievous sore: it shall not rest,
> But like some pestilent man toss in thy breast.
> . . . . .
> [to Hippolito] Now with thy dagger
> Nail down his tongue, and mine shall keep possession
> About his heart.
> . . . . .
> If he but wink, not brooking the foul object,
> Let our two other hands tear up his lids
> And make his eyes like comets shine through blood.
> (171–74, 192–98)

Such strong stuff is surely meant to startle even the less squeamish among us. But if Vindice's show mixes terror with its humor, both are in his control and all is presented through his commanding point of view. Any reaction against that view will have to come from an audience's predisposed resistance to it, a resistance that could find no supportive foothold in the scene itself. The presentation of Clarence's murder in *Richard III,* where the victim is given ample sway over our sympathy and our horror at the "bloody deed" is voiced by the recanting Second Murderer, provides an illustrative contrast here (act 1, scene 4), as would the blinding of Gloucester in *King Lear,* where our pity and outrage are given vent through the reaction of Cornwall's servants (act 3, scene 7).[9] No opposing voices and no un- conscious ironies in Vindice's own lines offer a comparable counterforce to his triumph in this scene or give us any ground on which to question his own assessment that "when the bad bleeds, then is the tragedy good" (199). The Duke (not a Clarence, of course, let alone a Gloucester), even when his tongue is not "nailed" into silence, manages only brief groans that Vindice and Hippolito convert into straight lines for their vaunting gibes:

> *Duke*: My teeth are eaten out.
> *Vind*:   Hadst any left?
> ·   ·   ·   ·   ·
> *Duke*:   O, my tongue!
> *Vind*: Your tongue? 'twill teach you to kiss closer,
>   Not like a slobbering Dutchman.
> (158–62)

Spurio and the Duchess, bent on their own revenge against the Duke, are made unconscious puppets dancing to Vindice's controlling tune here. And the solid, Horatio-like figure of Hippolito is emphatically supportive of Vindice's every move:

> Brother, I do applaud thy constant vengeance,
> The quaintness of thy malice, above thought.
> (107–8)

That response, applauding quaint malice, epitomizes our engagement with mischievous knavery at its most winning. Here the insistent violence of the malice may startle us as much as its wit entertains us. But violence is framed in wit as Vindice closes out the scene by inviting us to smile sardonically with him at the decorum of the banquet music that covers the Duke's final scream:

> *Duke*: I cannot brook—   [Vindice *kills him*]
> *Vind*:   The brook is turn'd to blood.
> *Hipp*: Thanks to loud music.
> *Vind*:   'Twas our friend indeed.
>   'Tis state in music for a duke to bleed.
> (216–18)

Whether or not we can be comfortable with him in such a pointedly bloody jest, Vindice now takes complete command of the action, and nothing is allowed to compete with his knavish presentation of it. The only other compelling voice in this scene has been Vindice's own when he takes time out from his "antic amble" to meditate on mortal folly once more from the skull's grimly satiric vantage point (68–97); but I would like to defer my account of that shift in tone and perspective for the moment. The primary shift here, in any case, is that which gives Vindice such sure ascendancy. From this point on, the play and our view of it are (like the "slavish duke") "in the hands of knaves": of Vindice, that is, and his faultless partner, Hippolito (3.5.156–57).

Those faulty partners Ambitioso and Supervacuo continue to serve as foolish foils, setting off the successful revengers through a series of pointed juxtapositions. Having seen Vindice wield Gloriana's skull with such grotesque artistry to bring down the old Duke, we then see the Duchess's sons put down by the severed head of the "wrong" brother (act 3, scene 6). In act 4 successive scenes show us Ambitioso and Supervacuo (the latter with rapier drawn) gnashing their teeth in helpless frustration as they watch their mother brazenly "disgrace" them with her bastard paramour, and then Vindice and Hippolito putting their drawn daggers away under the "sweet shower" of their mother's repentant tears as they cure her of her court-spawned "disease" and restore her to "good thoughts" (act 4, scenes 3 and 4).[10] As this scene suggests, however, the most significant contrasts are not between the successful brothers and their foolish counterparts, but between the success now enjoyed by Vindice and Hippolito and their previous setbacks. Gratiana's conversion is the mirror image of her earlier corruption, and Vindice, who had suffered the shock of her easy fall with us, now directs her recovery to an outcome so joyous that it makes him momentarily forget his knavish business with Lussurioso (4.4.83–87). That business, however, is his main occupation in acts 4 and 5, and his adroit management of it reverses his early frustrations at court as surely as this scene sets his own house back in order.

The bedchamber debacle had, of course, worn out "Piato's" welcome with Lussurioso, so a new role is called for. As though to emphasize his new-found success, the former melancholic who had disguised himself as a knave now chooses (as he actually blossoms into a winning knave) the "role" of a melancholic to reenlist in Lussurioso's service under his own name. And Vindice now masters the man he "serves" at every turn. Apparent obstacles of the sort that earlier foiled the brothers' knavery now become activating stimuli for their facile wit. The "impossible task" of producing Piato alive is "well convey'd, / Upon a sudden wit" by Hippolito's excuse that the nonexistent pander is rendered unfit for Lussurioso's lordly presence by that "worst of all the deadly sins, . . . drunkenness" (a mighty claim for the prestige of drunkenness in *this* setting! [4.2.165–81]). And Vindice swiftly converts the equally impossible task of producing Piato's corpse into the "device" of dressing the dead Duke in Piato's clothes and thus resolving both mysteries of the pander's disappearance and the Duke's murder in one stroke. Vindice's response to Hippolito at the inception of this device epitomizes the movement from bewilderment to triumph that now characterizes their knavery:

> *Hipp*: Brother, we lose ourselves.
> *Vind*:   But I have found it.
>   'Twill hold, 'tis sure; thanks, thanks to any spirit
>   That mingled it 'mongst my inventions.
> (4.2.195–97)

Whereas earlier scenes were structured around Vindice's collapse from knavish bravado into "angry froth" (act 1, scene 3, and act 2, scene 1), sequences that now begin with Vindice either stymied (4.1.17–39) or chafing (5.1.14–20) end on a confident note:

> *Hipp*: Firmer and firmer.
> *Vind*:   Nay, doubt not 'tis in grain;
>   I warrant it hold color.
> (4.2.218–19)

> *Vind*: Ay, that's the word; we are firm yet;
>   Strike one strain more, and then we crown our wit.
> (5.1.158–59)

As Vindice's knavery grows "firmer and firmer" through these final acts, it also becomes easier for us to enjoy than his first violent triumph over the Duke had been. Several factors help to draw us into the fun he has now and allow us to applaud the quaintness of his malice without balking at the malice of his quaintness. For one thing, Vindice's primary antagonist, Lussurioso, slips rapidly toward the buffoonish level of his bumbling stepbrothers, and the scenes he shares with Vindice align our laughter at his comic villainy with the revenger's consistently superior view. As in other respects, reversals from the patterns of earlier scenes enforce this alignment. Whereas Vindice's first job interview as Piato tended to expose him somewhat comically as a mere "puny" in Lussurioso's wicked world (act 1, scene 3), he controls the second one entirely, and it is Lussurioso who here betrays signs of vulnerable naiveté in his straight lines ("May it be possible such men should breathe?"; "It seems most strange to me" [4.2.56, 64]). Whereas Lussurioso now exposes himself to our derision by boasting foolishly in an aside of his "deep policy" (4.2.187), Vindice's asides, once anguished outcries, become steady guides to our amusement at the success of his device. So perfectly do Lussurioso and the lesser courtlings fall into their parts in Vindice's plot that he can virtually stand apart and watch the show with us. Of the fourteen speeches assigned to him through the latter half of act 5, scene 1, thirteen are spoken aside to Hippolito and us while his plan "hits / Past the apprehension of indifferent wits" (125–26). As Lussurioso complains, the Vindice whom he earlier took for an easily managed tool villain now "proves a knave" indeed (4.1.13). And since the dramatic emphasis throughout these scenes is on his wit and his victims' folly, his knavery offers us more to laugh at and less to be shocked by than it had in the Duke's violent demise.

There is violence, to be sure, in the final acts, rather more than less of it as the body count accelerates rapidly toward the end. But its presentation no longer stresses the pain inflicted on the victims as it did with the Duke. Instead, the emphasis on the jest or the neatness of the contrivance moves us (as was so frequently the case in *The Jew of Malta*) more to humor than to horror. The use of the Duke's disguised body as a prop in act 5, scene 1, where it substitutes for the drunken Piato ("So, so, he leans well"), recalls Barabas's farcical handling of the friars' murders in that earlier play. And the nicely choreographed masque in which Lussurioso and his fawning lords die, followed by the aborted second masque in which the remaining dukelings bring one another down like falling dominoes, provides a spectacle in which symmetrical dance and comic rigidity combine to preclude pity or terror. Such deaths, meted out so fittingly, can provide a high point in the knavish fun rather than spoiling it for us. It might be said that the movement from Vindice's more disturbing murder of the Duke to the "purer" sport of the final acts matches, in the second half of the play, the earlier movement from his uncomfortable opening speech to the broader humor of his first ventures in knavery; but the play's earlier humor tended to turn against him, whereas it now all flows his way.

It is not only the play's sport that carries us along with Vindice's growing momentum and encourages us to applaud his success through the final acts. We may have forgotten the group of right-minded lords who joined Hippolito in an early pledge to revenge the rape and consequent suicide of "that virtuous lady," Antonio's wife, a pledge that Antonio himself welcomed as his "comfort" (act 1, scene 4); but they now suddenly reappear, supported by "five hundred gentlemen," as colleagues in Vindice's scheme "to blast this villainous dukedom vex'd with sin," and they lend credence to Vindice's sense that it is no time to be fastidious about ways and means:

> *Vind*: My lords, be all of music;
>   Strike old griefs into other countries
>   That flow in too much milk and have faint livers,
>   Not daring to stab home their discontents.
> . . . . .
>   Wind up your souls to their full height again.
> *Piero*: How?
> *1st Lord*: Which way?
> *3rd Lord*:   Any way; our wrongs are such,
>   We cannot justly be reveng'd too much.
> (5.2.1–9)

Bolstered by this civic spirit, Vindice and Hippolito have the apparent sanction of heaven as well. Vindice's metaphorical identification of his cause with celestial fireworks ("Let our hid flames break out, as fire, as lightning" [5.2.5]) is visibly realized when "a blazing star appeareth" over Lussurioso's fatal corona-tion banquet (act 5, scene 3). The blatant contrast between this alignment and Lussurioso's ludicrous defiance of "that bushing-flaring star" (5.3.19) gives us every reason to suppose that Vindice correctly interprets the thunder that sounds when Lussurioso falls under his revenging sword:

No power is angry when the lustful die;
When thunder claps, heaven likes the tragedy.[11]
(5.3.47–48)

Given such thundering support for his cause, then, what are we
to make of the final twist in which Vindice is punished rather
than praised by Antonio, the beneficiary of his successful
revenge? Vindice's own cavalier response to this sudden turn
allows us to make less of it than we might, I believe. The
conclusion could force the troublesome issue of justifiable
revenge, of the rights and wrongs of a tyrannicide motivated by
legitimate grievances but carried out by duplicitous means—an
issue that the tragedy of the period could never comfortably
resolve. If this question were seriously posed, the play has
provided ample evidence for the comparative "innocence" of
Vindice's "villainy" that could be called on to justify our
engagement in his commanding point of view through the last
two acts. One could cite his motives: his abhorrence of the
rampant vices of the court he attacks and the freedom from
personal ambition that allows him to place the purged dukedom
in honest Antonio's "reverend" care. In defense of his knavish
means, one could point out the helpless vulnerability of those
more radically innocent targets of courtly corruption—Gloriana,
Antonio's "general honest Lady," and Castiza with her straight-
laced preference for "ordinary words" (1.2.46; 2.1.18)—and agree
with Vindice that to be honest is not to be (or at least not to be
effective) in this world (1.1.95). Surely no one who has
understood or enjoyed this play at all can be asked to see its
concluding action through Antonio's totally innocent eyes, a view
not only incapable of wit or irony, but blind to distinctions
between the apparently well-meaning fourth lord and a "foul
monster," or between himself and his lecherous predecessors as
potential victims of Vindice's murderous schemes (5.3.69, 103).[12]
The defense of Vindice would have to contend, of course, not
only with whatever predisposition against extralegal regicide
refused to be quelled in the minds of the audience, but with the
shocking presentation of Vindice's rough justice against the old
Duke. But momentum since that scene has swung so fully the
revenger's way that Antonio's sudden sentence might well be

countered with a defense that, if it did not totally vindicate the play's knavish hero, could plausibly claim that he is at worst an "innocent villain" after all.

Such an argument is rendered not so much invalid as unnecessary by Vindice's concluding speech. Any audience, and surely a Jacobean one, could be made profoundly uncomfortable were they asked here to reflect seriously on the full moral implications of Vindice's revenge and their own responses to it. In the bitter twists of his opening soliloquy and the painful violence of his first revenge, Vindice has shown his capacity to unsettle us, to make us uncomfortable even with his knavery's most stunning triumph. But now, in his final "downfall," he allows us to enjoy a retrospective view of that knavery in his own sportive mood, with no troublesome reflections. He does so by turning at once from the potentially disturbing question of "conscience" (106) and placing both his triumph and his fall in artistic terms that emphasize its poetic (rather than moral or legal) justice. Even more surely than Volpone, he proves most winning in his ultimate defeat and takes final custody of the play by setting the tone of its conclusion. It is a bright, witty tone, lightened by the crisp couplets that seal Vindice's approval of his dramatically decorous punishment:

> Are we not reveng'd?
> Is there one enemy left alive amongst those?
> 'Tis time to die, when we are ourselves our foes.

He recalls an earlier "knavish sentence" about murderers revealing their own crimes and thus claims as his own the irony that would otherwise tell against him by capping it with a jest.[13] Disdaining to spoil his play's perfectly achieved form with superfluous slaughter, he declares himself "well" and bids us adieu in an exit line aimed at applause of a hearty sort that would be inappropriate for the "piteous tragedy" honest Antonio supposes has taken place (60):

> And now, my lord, since we are in forever:
> This work was ours, which else might have been slipp'd;
> And if we list, we could have nobles clipp'd
> And go for less than beggars; but we hate

> To bleed so cowardly. We have enough,
> I'faith, we're well: our mother turn'd, our sister true,
> We die after a nest of dukes—adieu.

Vindice thus carries us through the potential dilemma of an appropriate moral response to his actions without calling our attention to it. Lest we be disturbed by the play's acquiescence in his crimes, Vindice is punished; and lest we be dejected by the punishment of one whose sport has engaged us increasingly through these final scenes, Vindice accepts his fate with a knavish brio and cavalier grace that encourage us to applaud him cheerfully at the end. If he is so pleased, why should we worry?[14]

Vindice can in fact afford to be pleased despite the "speedy execution" awaiting him offstage. Unlike our other knave-heroes, he has achieved exactly what he intended. If his final boast to Antonio that Lussurioso's murder was "witty carried" and "well manag'd" proves fatally indiscreet, it is nonetheless perfectly justified. Other knaves fall short of their goals by getting caught in their own contrivances, but Vindice had no goal beyond destroying the "nest of dukes." "Strike one strain more," he urged Hippolito before the deadly revels, "and then we crown our wit" (5.1.159). Since that crown was the only one he aimed at, he can take final satisfaction in his attainment of it and leave "the hope of Italy" in innocent Antonio's unappreciative hands. Thus, alone among our knaves, he has progressed from fret to sport, reversing Richard's more characteristically villainous path.

But if Vindice is no longer "sighing o'er death's vizard" (1.1.50) as he leaves, his initial understanding of the skull's lesson may serve the blithe spirit of his last farewell. His first call to knavery had been sparked by that "shell of death" and "terror to fat folks" with which he was on such easy and familiar terms. As his "studies' ornament," the skull may have fostered Vindice's immunity to the lust that makes Lussurioso and his father more slaves than knaves and to the ambition that sets the Duchess's elder sons at one another's throats behind each other's backs. On the verge of his first spectacular success, Vindice had interrupted his "throng of happy apprehensions" with a full-blown meditation on the skull:

> 　　　　　　　　　　　　　Here's an eye,
> Able to tempt a great man—to serve God;
> A pretty hanging lip, that has forgot now to dissemble;
> Methinks this mouth should make a swearer tremble,
> A drunkard clasp his teeth and not undo 'em
> To suffer wet damnation to run through 'em.
> (3.5.54–59)

If detached wit seems in control of these spruce couplets, the
voice soon turns reflective and probing:

> And now methinks I could e'en chide myself
> For doting on her beauty.
> ·　·　·　·　·
> Does the silkworm expend her yellow labors
> For thee? for thee does she undo herself?
> Are lordships sold to maintain ladyships
> For the poor benefit of a bewitching minute?
> ·　·　·　·　·
> Surely we're all mad people, and they
> Whom we think are, are not.
> (68–80)

　　As I suggested earlier, Vindice's larger awareness of mortality's
ironies may be his most telling advantage as a knave, and he
forces that awareness directly upon us here:

> 　　　　　　　　　　　It were fine, methinks,
> To have thee seen at revels, forgetful feasts,
> And unclean brothels; sure, 'twould fright the sinner
> And make him a good coward, put a reveler
> Out of his antic amble,
> And cloy an epicure with empty dishes.
> Here might a scornful and ambitious woman
> Look through and through herself.—See, ladies, with false
> 　　forms
> You deceive men, but cannot deceive worms.—
> Now to my tragic business.
> (89–98)

This last abrupt turn back to the scheme in hand could suggest a disjunction between Vindice's scopic meditative vision and his present action. After such knowledge, what vengeance? Why should the knave not be put out of his "antic amble" as well as the reveler when he sees that they are both ultimately caught up in the same dance of death?[15]

Vindice could reasonably argue, however, that his knavery never serves any worldly goal that would be invalidated by the skull and that his vengeance forces the very lesson of his meditation on those whose vicious lives have heeded it least. Surely the belated realization of that lesson is reflected painfully in the Duke's "affrighted eyeballs" as the object of Vindice's meditation and the grotesque wit of his knavish scheme converge:

> *Vind*:   Duke, dost know
> Yon dreadful vizard? View it well; 'tis the skull
> Of Gloriana, whom thou poisoned'st last.
> *Duke*: O, 'tas poisoned me.
> . . . . . .
> *Vind*:   The very ragged bone
> Has been sufficiently reveng'd.
> (3.5.145–52)

Vindice's insistence on sharing his death's head and its message with us ("See, ladies . . .") may, like his more violent antics, make us uncomfortable; but full acquiescence in his vision, for those who can manage it, need not be accompanied by a long face or a "grave look." Vindice's own sense of fun is nourished by his awareness of mortality. His detachment from worldly desires (apart from those that are satisfied by the success of his schemes in themselves) allows Vindice to approximate pure knavery, just as enslavement to them draws the old Duke into his trap. And if he has made us uneasy at times, that same detachment nonetheless supports the amazing grace with which he accepts his final punishment and thereby eases us past the prickly moral questions that our engagement in his knavery might otherwise raise. Fully knowing its inevitability in any case, he can freely jest his doom, unlike the lust-driven Youngest Son who dies cursing his baffled brothers, and in even sharper contrast to Lussurioso, who feeds toward the end on absurd hopes of immortality (1.2.49; 3.6.43–51; 5.3.34–35). It is true that Vindice is pleased with his accomplishments in this world as he leaves it and that, after the fret and the frustrations of his earlier efforts, he takes pride in the perfect achievements of his riper wit. But we may also see in the merry tone of his final speech this knave's last bow to what he has known all along to be the superior irony of the grinning skull.[16]

Conclusion

The four of a kind drawn together here in their varying suits and colors do not, of course, represent a full survey of knavery in English Renaissance drama. They do, however, stand out from their fellows in ways that are important to my subject. Though knaves abound in plays of this period, other candidates for inclusion here were left behind in the unruly heap of notes and drafts sloughed off by this slender book either because they do not dominate our view of the stages on which they perform or because the question of our engagement with them is less fruitfully challenging than is the case with these four—because, that is, they speak less provocatively to this book's central interest in dramatic point of view.

In a broader review of the field, the knaves who serve as presenters and contrivers of those three festive "school" pieces— *Jack Juggler, Ralph Roister Doister,* and *Gammer Gurton's Needle*—might well claim their places as forerunners of my four principals. Jack, Matthew Merrygreek, and Diccon all share with the Vice of the popular moralities both their prominence in their plays and the hall-based habit of interacting with us and making our responses to them a part of their show. But their creators found no need to make such interactions the occasions for our rejection of the knaves' inviting leads, as the morality playwrights had consistently done, since in these three cases knavish sport was carefully cleansed of the dangerous implications that clung to our participation in the Vice's mischievous mood. If there is nothing problematic about the fun we share with these three knaves, however, they anticipate my foursome not only in their antic scheming but in the focal control they are given over our view of the plots they initiate.

Since this convenient and effective structure, in which a central schemer introduces and presides over the play's action, was so widely shared among both "learned" and popular plays of the earlier Elizabethan period, it is perhaps surprising that so few plays of Shakespeare's time make full use of it. We find it embedded almost everywhere *within* plots and subplots and individual scenes, but the four plays discussed in this book are distinctive in their thoroughgoing adoption of it. Jonson's other great knave play resembles *Volpone* in this respect, of course. But after their opening (and mutually damaging) quarrel, we see much less of Face and Subtle in their own persons "backstage" than we do of Volpone and Mosca. As the whirligig of dupes being ushered on and off accelerates through *The Alchemist*, we appreciate the performance without developing any very close relationship with the two main contrivers of it. In any case, Face eludes the final condemnation that links Volpone with the other knaves included here and that would make full and sustained engagement with any of them a theatrical problem.

Since my larger concern is not knavery, after all, but dramatic point of view, it extends well beyond this book's particular focus. It should be safe to say that if this approach were applied more widely to English Renaissance drama, it would show more about multiple perspectives (as in my sketchy introductory remarks about *The Spanish Tragedy*) and concentrate less on single figures than my essays on these four works do. Some plays of the period, of course, feature Marlovian titans who tower over the crowds around them. And perhaps even more interestingly for such an approach, some plays are structured around nonknavish characters (Prospero, Vincentio, Altofronto / Malevole) whose larger awareness helps to give them something like the dramatist's shaping control over both the outcome of the action and our view of it. The norm of the age's drama, however, is a multiplicity and variety of focus through which our view of any one character, even those who are most important to us, is modified or mediated by others who also demand our attention. Often, and in the nature of the case, characters who stand somewhat aside from the center have a more openly directive effect on our point of view than the highlighted principals themselves. Nor need such directive characters be mere choruses. Enobarbus comes to mind, for example, and in the perplexed instances of Webster's tragedies, a study of point of view might find its greatest interest in the audience's relationship with Bosola and with Flamineo. But nowhere in the period is our interest focused more intensely through characters who manage both to be at the center of the action and to attempt a directive presenter's overview of it than in the four plays discussed here.

Finally, I would like to make some claims for the value of my approach that will, I hope, have been at least partially validated by my use of it here and should apply beyond this group of plays and their age to the study of drama in general. Like any other particular way of thinking about drama, the emphasis on point of view will be more interesting and instructive for some plays than for others, but our insight into any play must gain from attention to the ways in which it directs our attitude toward the characters in action, engaging us with or detaching us from their own ways of seeing. If some plays either don't allow their characters to address and interact with us so openly as my four knaves do, or don't allow us to enjoy knavish mischief so freely as these four plays do, that is a significant fact about the way they shape our understanding. The degree to which Molière contains and places Tartuffe within the guiding perspectives of characters whose view of him we can trust, for example, makes our detached understanding of that impostor simpler in kind than the one Jonson prompts us to adopt as we watch Volpone go into action; and a comparative study of the control over our view allowed to rogues and schemers in comedies from Aristophanes through the Restoration would be one plausible extension of this book's subject. Or, looking further ahead, as modern drama has deliberately broken through the illusion of reality that Ibsen attempted to establish and has drawn once again on the full resources of theatricalism's open interactions with the audience, a study of the ways in which the relationships its characters establish with us resemble or differ from those analyzed in this book should be rewarding. Surely, as the characters' control over "plot" diminishes in more recent plays, the *kind* of engagement a theatrically commanding knave can naturally evoke must diminish as well. But are we allowed to detach ourselves from fallible characters who expose themselves to our "considerate eyes" on the modern stage as readily as we could from Richard or Volpone in their lapses, or from their more foolish dupes? To what extent does modern theatricalism, rather than establishing hierarchies of awareness that distinguish the superior viewpoint (onstage and off) from the inferior, confuse whatever lines we might prefer to draw between our "reality" and the play's "fiction" and deny whatever elevation we might prefer to maintain over the helpless and hapless characters we watch? Situated in the "bog" Estragon sees when he turns our way and waiting futilely along with him for a Godot we will never see or know, can we still attain, even in the temporary sanctuary of the theater, anything resembling the secure and lofty overview of "God's spies"?

The larger reach I am suggesting here far exceeds my immediate grasp; and the questions just posed are not simply rhetorical, nor should they imply simple answers or simplistic distinctions (Marlowe may have been no more flattering to *The Jew's* audience than Beckett is to *Godot's*; and Shakespeare may tease us into more profound questions about the relationship between life's "reality" and a play's "fiction" than Pirandello does). These are questions, however, that could be fruitfully addressed through a focus on dramatic point of view and the ways in which it works to engage or detach us as we watch a play. If I ask more than I can answer here, that does not delimit the value of my approach, but only the extent of my accomplishment through it. In the Introduction, I acknowledge that the task of tracing engagement and detachment would be complicated by the presence of characters who draw more powerfully on our deeper feelings than any in these four plays do. That is so, but I do not want to suggest thereby that any attempt to take such characters and such feelings into account through a study of point of view would not be worth the effort. Exploring the factors that distinguish our views of Iago or Edmund in their plays from our view of Richard (their kindred spirit in so many ways) in his would be a natural move in that direction from my starting point here. And the value of that exploration should emerge from the fact that any distinction made between Iago or Edmund and those they destroy would not depend only on the qualities *in* the characters themselves, but also on the ways we are made to see and respond to them. How we are *involved* in making the distinction, and how we are thus made to "see it feelingly" as we experience the play, then become the critical focus.

It is the way in which that focus on our interaction with a play enhances our appreciative understanding of it that I want to stress in conclusion. In the case of *Richard III,* attention to the dynamics of our relationship with the presiding knave helps to explain why a play that does not really offer much challenging complexity for interpretation nonetheless holds such interest for us. *What* we should think is scarcely a problem here, but the art with which Shakespeare engages us theatrically and then steers us toward a "proper" view surely merits our study. On the other hand, actual complexities in *The Jew of Malta* and *The Revenger's Tragedy* can be too easily smoothed away by a sifting of thematic content that ignores the theatrical dynamics of our point of view. Ferneze may be "like" Barabas and Spurio may be "like" Vindice in important respects, but there are equally important differences in our views of them that prompt us to detach ourselves (for not very wholesome reasons) from the Jew and to engage ourselves with one revenger rather than the other. Showing these differences, as I hope my study has done, emphasizes the dramatic life of a play as we experience it rather than treating it as a thesis on policy or revenge. But emphasis on this theatrical dimension does not leave whatever ideas or values a play may offer us out of account. It should, rather, make our participation in or rejection of the various values represented in the action—including the value of theatrical enjoyment itself, on which the four knaves featured here play in such intriguing ways—a central part of our critical understanding.

Notes

References in the text and notes are to act, scene, and line (e.g., 3.2.14) or to scene and line (e.g., 2.156).

Introduction

1 The phrase is Vindice's in *The Revenger's Tragedy*, 3.5.156.

2 Robert Scholes and Robert Kellogg, *The Nature of Narrative* (New York: Oxford University Press, 1966), p. 240. On the other hand, Fredson Bowers claims that "most laws of drama that are not concerned with simple stagecraft have as their object the manipulation of the audience's point of view." Bowers's brief development of this thesis, which focuses on plot and its "climax as the key to point of view," differs considerably from my analysis. See "Shakespeare's Art: The Point of View," in *Literary Views: Critical and Historical Essays,* ed. Carroll Camden (Chicago: University of Chicago Press, 1964), pp. 45–58.

3 Bertrand Evans offers a systematic account of Shakespeare's use of hierarchies of awareness in *Shakespeare's Comedies* (Oxford: The Clarendon Press, 1960). Klaus Peter Jochum argues with some of Evans's premises in *Discrepant Awareness: Studies in English Renaissance Drama* (Frankfurt am Main: Peter Lang, 1979).

4 Brian Vickers presents a useful analysis of the effect of asides and soliloquies on the audience's point of view in "Shakespeare's Hypocrites," *Daedalus* 108 (1979): 45–83. Like many other commentators, however, Vickers stresses the engaging effect of these devices without noting that they are also frequently used to expose the speaker to our judgment or ridicule.

5 Maynard Mack provides the essential foundation for any discussion of this topic in "Engagement and Detachment in Shakespeare's Plays," in *Essays on Shakespeare and Elizabethan Drama in Honor of Hardin Craig,* ed. Richard Hosley (Columbia: University of Missouri Press, 1962), pp. 275–96.

6 Robert Heilman notes the general unsatisfactoriness of the term "identification" in a discussion of what I would call our engagement with Macbeth, but

I don't think that the new term he suggests, "conscentience," would help to clarify my argument. See "The Criminal as Tragic Hero: Dramatic Methods," *ShS* 19 (1966): 12–24.

7   Waldo F. McNeir, "The Masks of Richard the Third," *SEL* 11 (1971): 167–86.

8   Hugh M. Richmond, *Shakespeare's Political Plays* (New York: Random House, 1967), p. 180.

9   *Volpone, or The Fox,* ed. Jonas A. Barish (New York: Appleton-Century-Crofts, 1958), p. x.

10 Stephen Wigler, "If Looks Could Kill: Fathers and Sons in *The Revenger's Tragedy,*" *CompD* 9 (1975): 206–25.

11 Insofar as I "consider the play as a dynamic interaction between artist and audience" and "talk about the process of our involvement rather than our considered view after the aesthetic event," my approach attempts to meet some needs suggested in Norman Rabkin's Introduction to *Shakespeare and the Problem of Meaning* (Chicago: University of Chicago Press, 1981), p. 27. Whatever the pitfalls of such an approach, it tries to avoid those pointed out by Richard Levin in *New Readings vs. Old Plays* (Chicago: University of Chicago Press, 1979). Among the many recent studies of English Renaissance drama that offer clear precedents for the method attempted here are: Stephen Booth, "On the Value of Hamlet," in *Reinterpretations of Elizabethan Drama,* ed. Norman Rabkin (New York: Columbia University Press, 1969), pp. 137–76; Janet Adelman, *The Common Liar: An Essay on "Antony and Cleopatra"* (New Haven: Yale University Press, 1973); E.A.J. Honigmann, *Shakespeare: Seven Tragedies* (London: Macmillan, 1976); and two of Jean Howard's essays, "Shakespearean Counterpoint: Stage Technique and the Interaction Between Play and Audience," *SQ* 30 (1979): 343–57, and "Figures and Grounds: Shakespeare's Control of Audience Perception and Response," *SEL* 20 (1980): 185–99.

12 Rolf Soellner raises the questions that should disturb any easy assumptions about a hypothetical audience in a review article, "Two Studies of Audience Response," *SQ* 28 (1977): 366–69.

13 As with "point of view," the idea of an "implied audience" (or reader) has been much more fully developed in discussions of fiction than in those of drama. I don't think it is necessary to endorse or transpose the theoretical arguments of Stanley Fish or Wolfgang Iser in their entirety in order to make my point here, however. Janet Adelman says what I mean concisely and effectively: "A play must teach us how to see it" (*The Common Liar,* p. 11).

14 "Knave" had, of course, wider application for Elizabethans as a term of abuse or disparagement, but the sense in which I use it here—a crafty, mischievous schemer—was common. Stephen Gosson offers outraged testimony to knavery's theatrical appeal: "In the Theaters they generally take vp a wonderfull laughter, and shout altogether with one voyce, when they see some notable cosenedge practised, or some slie conueighance of baudry brought out of Italy. Whereby they showe them selues rather to like it then to rebuke it." N. W. Bawcutt cites this passage from *Plays Confuted in Five Actions* (1582) with reference to the "attractive villainy" of three of my

knaves—Richard III, Barabas, and Volpone—in his Revels edition of *The Jew of Malta* (Manchester: Manchester University Press, 1978), p. 26.

15 The reversal of priorities where pleasure and profit are concerned is one thing that makes Quomodo, Volpone's "citizen" counterpart in Middleton's *Michaelmas Term*, a less engaging knave: "Know, then, I have not spent this long vacation / Only for pleasure's sake. Give me the man / Who out of recreation culls advantage" (1.1.93–95).

16 For a fuller version of this argument, see my "Dangerous Sport: The Audience's Engagement with Vice in the Moral Interludes," *RenD* n.s. 6 (1973): 45–64.

17 *Shakespeare's Festive Comedy* (Princeton: Princeton University Press, 1959), pp. 8–9.

18 *The Dramatic Writings of Ulpian Fulwell*, ed. John S. Farmer (London: Early English Drama Society, 1906), pp. 4–5.

19 *The Castle of Perseverance*, ll. 519–25, in *The Macro Plays*, ed. Mark Eccles, Early English Text Society, no. 262 (London: Oxford University Press, 1969).

20 *Nice Wanton*, ll. 457–58, in *Specimens of the Pre-Shaksperean Drama*, ed. John M. Manly (1877; reprint, New York: Dover Publications, 1967).

21 Citations from *The Macro Plays*.

22 *The Trial of Treasure*, in Robert Dodsley's *Select Collection of Old English Plays*, ed. W. C. Hazlitt (1874–76; reprint, New York: B. Blom, 1964), 3:279.

23 The continuity between morality plays and Elizabethan drama is substantially documented in different ways by Bernard Spivack, *Shakespeare and the Allegory of Evil* (New York: Columbia University Press, 1958), and David M. Bevington, *From "Mankind" to Marlowe* (Cambridge: Harvard University Press, 1962). Spivack's focus is on the Vice.

24 *Shakespeare and the Popular Tradition in the Theater: Studies in the Social Dimension of Dramatic Form and Function*, ed. Robert Schwartz (Baltimore: Johns Hopkins University Press, 1978), p. 213. For *platea* and *locus*, see pp. 73–85.

25 Ibid., p. 256.

26 Weimann himself offers a brief analysis of Richard, ibid., pp. 159–60. Since my manuscript was completed, Michael E. Mooney has published a study of *The Revenger's Tragedy* that applies Weimann's theory systematically to Vindice's "*figurenposition*, or the correlation of his stage location with the 'speech, action and degree of stylization associated with that position' " (" 'This Luxurious Circle': *Figurenposition* in *The Revenger's Tragedy*," *ELR* 13 [1983], 162–81). Mooney stresses, as I do, the "theatrical *transaction* in which an actor actively engages himself with his audience"; and although I believe that transaction and our consequent "multi-consciousness" or "privileged awareness" work in a more fluid, less mechanical way than Mooney's analysis of "the correlation between voice and location" implies (his stage almost seems a chessboard sometimes as "Vindice moves from *platea* to *locus* and back again" and as "we easily slide in and out of the dramatic illusion with him" [173]), his essay surely complements mine.

27 *Lamb's Criticism*, ed. E. M. W. Tillyard (Cambridge; Cambridge University

Press, 1923), p. 51; Tillyard, *Shakespeare's History Plays* (New York: Macmillan, 1946), pp. 208–9.

28 *The Mirror up to Nature: The Technique of Shakespeare's Tragedies* (San Marino, Calif.: The Huntington Library, 1965), p. 95.

29 *The Cease of Majesty: A Study of Shakespeare's History Plays* (London: Arnold, 1961), p. 215.

30 See, for example, A. P. Rossiter's lively lecture, published as the title essay in *Angel With Horns,* ed. Graham Storey (London: Longmans, Green, 1961), pp. 1–22; and Murray Krieger, "The Dark Generations of *Richard III,*" *Criticism* 1 (1959): 32–48.

31 *The Dramatist and the Received Idea* (Cambridge: Cambridge University Press, 1968).

32 Ibid., pp. 75, 76; French, "The World of *Richard III,*" *ShakS* 4 (1968): 25–39.

33 Even a reading that agrees with mine so far as to see Richard as a play master ultimately caught in the irony of a larger providential play beyond his control arrives at its skeptical view of the final image of Providence by its own reflective reasoning rather than from any clearly pointed directives in the dialogue: "Richard was after all in a play within a play, and the real director was providence, now revealed as a Jester; providence employs Richard, mocks Richard, and—in the end—looks like Richard." That equation might, on consideration, seem justifiable; but nowhere is it suggested to the audience watching the play by images of Providence's leering smile or humped back. See Phillip Mallett, "Shakespeare's Trickster-Kings: Richard III and Henry V," in *The Fool and the Trickster: Studies in Honour of Enid Welsford,* ed. Paul V. A. Williams (Cambridge: D. S. Brewer, 1979), p. 71.

34 John Bakeless, *The Tragicall History of Christopher Marlowe* (Cambridge: Harvard University Press, 1942), 1:329.

35 *Suffering and Evil in the Plays of Christopher Marlowe* (Princeton: Princeton University Press, 1962), p. 125. G. K. Hunter also openly addresses the problem by asserting that the use of allusions in *The Jew* "implies an ideal audience that . . . can judge the hero by his understanding of the texts he uses": "The Theology of *The Jew of Malta,*" *JWCI* 27 (1964): 211–40. My own sense is that this play is less flattering about the audience it implies.

36 *Imago, Zeitschrift für Anwendung der Psychoanalyse auf die Geisteswissenschaften IV,* 6 (1916): 320; quoted in Wolfgang Clemen, *A Commentary on Shakespeare's "Richard III,"* trans. Jean Bonheim (London: Methuen, 1968), p. 7, n. 1. In a 1977 Stratford, Ontario production, Brian Bedford made the audience feel the inner pain of his Richard from his first entrance and gave one hapless spectator, who dared to laugh at the first mention of Richard's "rudely stamped" shape, a severe lesson in "fellow feeling" by fixing him with a long, chilling stare. It was a superb use of actor-audience dynamics for a particular effect, and the performance was first-rate throughout, but the result was, I believe, a rather different play than Shakespeare's text (or the best approximation of it we have) presents.

37 See Arthur Colby Sprague, *Shakespeare's Histories: Plays for the Stage* (London: Society for Theatre Research, 1964), for an account of *Richard III*

in the theater. Sprague concurs with a reviewer who worried that Olivier aimed at the wrong sort of laughter in this role, remarking that "such laughter as Richard causes should be uneasy" (p. 135). Of course it *should* be, if decent human conduct is uppermost in question, but I don't believe the play always *makes* us uneasy about sharing Richard's fun. The question of the relationship between text and performance is especially vexed in this play's case, both by uncertainties about an authoritative original text and by Cibber's stage version, which still holds partial sway in Olivier's film. On both counts, see Anthony Hammond's introduction to his New Arden edition (London: Methuen, 1981).

1   *Richard III*

1   *Richard III* (4.1.53–55). Citations are from G. Blakemore Evans's edition in *The Complete Pelican Shakespeare,* ed. Alfred Harbage (Baltimore: Penguin Books, 1969).

2   Other critics have suggested something very like this movement from engagement to detachment, but even those who focus most directly on the handling of perspective tend to look at the play structurally as a whole rather than progressively as a developing experience. Larry S. Champion, in *Perspective in Shakespeare's English Histories* (Athens: University of Georgia Press, 1980), though he does note the change in our view of Richard toward the end, bases his argument that "Richard provides the eye . . . through which the spectator observes the action" largely on a catalog of the number of soliloquies, asides, lines, and appearances through which Richard "dominates the stage" (p. 61). Nicholas Brooke's fine essay in *Shakespeare's Early Tragedies* (London: Methuen, 1968) shows how the "opening out of successively larger patterns one from within another" in the play modifies our view of the clash between Richard's vital energy and the fixed moral order (p. 72). Again, however, his emphasis is more on "the structural shape" of the play seen whole.

3   As others have noticed, *Richard III* is unique among Shakespeare's plays in its use of this sort of opening, where the central figure presents himself and the play to us in a soliloquy.

4   No lecturer could now speak, as A. P. Rossiter did, of theatrical talent as "an aspect of Richard's appeal which has . . . passed relatively unexamined" (*Angel With Horns,* p. 16). Along with Rossiter's, Anne Righter's initiative should be credited here, though more for the general concern with theatricalism that has followed her lead in *Shakespeare and the Idea of the Play* (London: Chatto and Windus, 1962) than for her analysis of Richard himself in these terms. She surely oversimplifies Richard's case when she says that he "appears in a dazzling series of roles, all of which are completely successful. Through five long acts he manages to deceive virtually everyone around him" (p. 97). Ralph Berry may overstate the opposite case when he "corrects" Righter by saying that Richard "deceives hardly anyone" (*The Shakespearean Metaphor: Studies in Language and Form* [London:

Macmillan, 1978], p. 118, n. 17). Like Berry, Michael Neill sees Richard's early success and ultimate failure in terms of his acting, and, interestingly for my thesis about these four knaves, remarks in passing that "Richard's delight in his prowess as an actor, the bustling energy of his performances," is "the same quality that stirs us in a Barabbas [*sic*], a Volpone, or a Vindice" ("Shakespeare's Halle of Mirrors: Play, Politics, and Psychology in *Richard III*," *ShakS* 8 [1975]: 99–129). Even more closely approximating my argument about Richard, though with more exclusive focus on his acting, are those set forth by Waldo F. McNeir, "The Masks of Richard the Third," *SEL* 11 (1971): 167–86; and Thomas van Laan, *Role-Playing in Shakespeare* (Toronto: University of Toronto Press, 1978), pp. 137–47.

5 Several studies note, along with Richard himself, Richard's likeness to the morality Vice (e.g., Spivack, *Shakespeare and the Allegory of Evil*); and several remark that we may be made uneasy by our enjoyment of his villainy (e.g., McNeir, "The Masks of Richard the Third"). None, so far as I know, stresses an important difference between Richard's relationship to us and the Vice's—the fact that Richard does *not* call open attention to our engagement with him. Also, in the absence of such open interaction, none indicates *how* we are made uneasy by that relationship or how we are made conscious of its implications.

6 The analogy with Romeo and Juliet is noted by Edward I. Berry, *Patterns of Decay: Shakespeare's Early Histories* (Charlottesville: University of Virginia Press, 1975), p. 79.

7 Jean Howard points out the change in perspective here in "Shakespearean Counterpoint: Stage Technique and the Interaction between Play and Audience," *SQ* 30 (1979): 348–50. The elimination of Margaret from the play, as in Cibber's version and Olivier's film, radically affects the developing relationship between our point of view and Richard's.

8 Like Tillyard, others who study *Richard III* in the context of the other history plays tend, perhaps naturally, to stress the larger or longer patterns that contain and place Richard's villainous actions, though not all agree with Tillyard's basic thesis. With significant variations, the following all emphasize the moral pattern within which Richard is properly destroyed: M. M. Reese, *The Cease of Majesty* (London: Arnold, 1961); Henry A. Kelly, *Divine Providence in the England of Shakespeare's Histories* (Cambridge: Harvard University Press, 1970); Robert B. Pierce, *Shakespeare's History Plays: The Family and the State* (Columbus: Ohio State University Press, 1971); and Berry, *Patterns of Decay*. Whereas I trace the effect of the emerging overview on our perspective, such studies tend to posit the larger moral pattern as *the* basic viewpoint for the play as a whole. Among book-length studies of the histories, Robert Ornstein's *A Kingdom for a Stage: The Achievement of Shakespeare's History Plays* (Cambridge: Harvard University Press, 1972) is notably "skeptical" in its departure from Tillyard's view. In his introduction, Ornstein argues that the "Tudor myth" is largely Tillyard's myth (pp. 14–19), and his acute discussion of Richard is more dramatically than historically oriented. Likewise, S. C. Sen Gupta, in

Shakespeare's Historical Plays (London: Oxford University Press, 1964), argues that "if . . . the plays are considered *as* plays, it will appear very doubtful whether Shakespeare was primarily interested in propagating any particular political or moral idea" (p. 181).

9   Emrys Jones stresses the effect our historical "foreknowledge" has on our view of the action in "Bosworth Eve," *EIC* 25 (1975): 38–54. This factor, when it comes into play, distinguishes Shakespeare's direction of our perspective in *Richard III* from the ways it can be played on in the other three dramas to be considered here, where an unknown story can (and does) take surprising turns.

10   *King Lear*, 3.7.24.

11   Shakespeare *could* have made us laugh with Richard at this heinous crime, as Dickens in fact did through Sam Weller's use of it to illustrate a homely proverb: "Business first, pleasure arterwards, as King Richard the Third said wen he stabbed the 'tother king in the Tower afore he smothered the babbies."

12   Bridget Lyons notes Richard's violation of the norms of "royal theatrics" in this sequence and others in " 'King's Games': Stage Imagery and Political Symbolism in *Richard III*," *Criticism* 20 (1978): 17–30.

13   The obtrusive parallelism of the wooing scenes is, of course, often noted in studies of the play, and most agree that the second is a marked comedown from the first, though some argue that Richard again triumphs brilliantly. For opposed readings, see Louis E. Dollarhide, "Two Unassimilated Movements of *Richard III*: An Interpretation," *Mississippi Quarterly* 14 (1960): 40–46; and Stephen L. Tanner, "Richard III versus Elizabeth: An Interpretation," *SQ* 24 (1973): 468–72.

14   Discussions of the change that takes place once Richard seizes power can illustrate the major difference between my approach and the numerous analyses of his "character," which range from studies of his relationship to such theatrical prototypes as the Senecan or Machiavellian villain (Clarence V. Boyer, *The Villain as Hero in Elizabethan Tragedy* [London: Routledge and Sons, 1914]) to essays that treat him as though he were a fascinatingly dangerous person rather than a conventional stage contrivance (John Palmer, *Political Characters of Shakespeare* [London: Macmillan, 1945]). I agree with those who see a change in character (or characterization), and I willingly take the general consensus that Richard is more "winning" before than after he gains the crown as support for my own reading; but I would add that our response to that change is strongly affected by the handling of our perspective on (and into) Richard—by the ways in which he either controls our view of a scene or is placed within it for us. This emphasis should give a further dimension to arguments such as that of William E. Sheriff, who ascribes our changing feelings to the change *in* Richard: "Shakespeare . . . removes any guilt we may feel in finding Richard sympathetic by presenting a different man in the final two acts. . . . Richard has developed from the brilliant comical villain of the first act to the befuddled, tragical murderer who blindly slays five 'Richmonds' at

Bosworth Field before being destroyed by the real Richmond" ("The Grotesque Comedy of *Richard III*," *SlitI* 5 [1972]: 51–64). S. C. Sen Gupta sees the change in characterization as such a radical one that the "character" of Richard splits into two discontinuous parts: "There is no inner connexion between the man who mocked conscience and the man who is now mocked by it" (*Shakespeare's Historical Plays*, p. 97). Probing into Richard's character as well as Shakespeare's characterization, Robert B. Heilman (whose analysis of Richard as a "picaro-type trickster" corresponds to my treatment of him as a knave) uses the analogy of postcoital lassitude to explain the schemer's loss of vital interest once his "goal" is attained ("Satiety and Conscience: Aspects of *Richard III*," *AR* 24 [1964]: 57–73). Whatever their particular arguments, these studies are all more interested in the character himself than in the ways in which our perspective on that character is directed.

15 An overwhelming majority of commentators see Richard recovering himself on the day of battle and thus ending on an upswing. I agree that he ends spectacularly, but insist that we watch (and may even admire) the spectacle from a very different angle than the one he had shared with us in his early performances.

2 Barabas

1 Harry Levin notes that Barabas has more lines than any other Marlovian character, "indeed, about half of the play": *The Overreacher: A Study of Christopher Marlowe* (Cambridge: Harvard University Press, 1952), p. 62. Citations from *The Jew of Malta* are from Richard W. Van Fossen's edition in the Regents Renaissance Drama Series (Lincoln: University of Nebraska Press, 1964).

2 As my wording here suggests, my interpretation of the "Marlovian twist" given to morality play tactics differs considerably from the one Douglas Cole offers in *Suffering and Evil in the Plays of Christopher Marlowe* (Princeton: Princeton University Press, 1962), p. 144.

3 David Bevington places Machiavel's Prologue as a "conventional morality device heralding the appearance of the unregenerate protagonist" and compares it to Satan's introduction of his vicious followers at the opening of *The Conflict of Conscience (From "Mankind" to Marlowe* [Cambridge: Harvard University Press, 1962], p. 222). True, Satan opens the first scene of *The Conflict of Conscience* thus; but an explanatory Prologue precedes and introduces *him* in the traditional morality manner.

4 Our response is not, however, written into the dialogue, as it customarily was in the moral interludes.

5 N. W. Bawcutt emphasizes this suggestion in his Revels edition of *The Jew of Malta* (Manchester: Manchester University Press, 1978) by placing a semicolon at the end of line 6; he comments on the implication in his introduction, p. 12.

6 As always, the "we" I speak of is the play's implied audience, which clearly

is expected here to share the Elizabethan prejudice against Jews exemplified by the Christians in *The Merchant of Venice.*

7 Bevington says that Barabas's "revelation in soliloquy of this hypocrisy is an ironic undercutting of the apparent tragedy for a comic purpose. It shows Barabas as the 'Vice,' who mockingly and boastfully reveals his strategy to his audience after having cheated them into misplaced sympathy" (*From "Mankind" to Marlowe,* p. 225). But the Vice's customary way, like that of other knaves who aim at a comic response, is to confide in the audience *first* and to let us share the joke of his "hypocrisy" with him.

8 The change in tone and substance from this point on in the play dismayed an earlier generation of scholars who had admired (and I believe half created) the Barabas of the early scenes as a Marlovian titan. C. F. Tucker Brooke declared the negative view of the change to be unanimous: "All critics of the play have noticed with regret the failure of the last half of *The Jew of Malta* to fulfill the splendid promise of the first two acts. It is beyond question [!] that the vigorous flow of tragic interest and character portrayal with which the play opens wastes away amid what . . . is a wilderness of melodrama and farce" (*The Works of Christopher Marlowe* [Oxford: The Clarendon Press, 1910], p. 232). The consensus that the play falls apart, or splits into two incompatible parts, held firm through the first half of this century in editions, studies of Marlowe's life and art (the latter always seen then, as it still tends to be, in the supposed image of the former), and general surveys of Elizabethan tragedy. A natural tendency for those who think the play breaks down is to posit either multiple authorship or corruption of the text, and the latter supposition has been abetted by the long gap between the play's initial performance (ca. 1590) and the surviving text's publica. on (1633). F. P. Wilson speaks for those who would attribute the Jew's alleged early grandeur to Marlowe's genius and his collapse into knavery to a hand or hands unknown: "To suppose that the same man who wrote the first two acts was wholly responsible for the last three is revolting to sense and sensibility, for these belong to a different world of art, if indeed they can be said to belong to the world of art at all" (*Marlowe and the Early Shakespeare* [Oxford: The Clarendon Press, 1953], p. 65). J. C. Maxwell, though he acknowledges the change in tone, has insisted in a pair of articles that assumptions about corruption or revision by other hands than Marlowe's cannot be based on very secure textual evidence ("The Assignment of Speeches in *The Jew of Malta,*" *MLR* 43 [1948]: 510–12; "How Bad is the Text of *The Jew of Malta?*", *MLR* 48 [1953]: 435–38). Most recent critics have treated the play as a fundamentally sound text, whatever their view of it. My own reading of it clearly considers the surprises it springs on us to be purposive, and I therefore gladly accept (without feeling qualified to judge) Maxwell's argument for textual integrity.

9 Though Douglas Cole's "Comic Accomplice in Elizabethan Revenge Tragedy," *RenD* 9 (1966): 125–39, takes essentially the same moral view of comic action in *The Jew* as did his *Suffering and Evil,* he acknowledges that Barabas and Ithamore form "less a sinister and threatening partnership than

a diabolical comedy team," so that "one almost looks forward to their antic evils" (p. 128).

10 It would be fair to say that the argument Howard Babb made for thematic unity through juxtaposition of Barabas's "policy" with that of the Christians has replaced the older concern over Barabas's "degeneration" as the orthodox view of the play, though Babb did not, of course, effect this transformation alone. Along with his "*Policy* in Marlowe's *The Jew of Malta*," *ELH* 24 (1957): 85–94, other representative accounts of the play's thematically coherent vision of a bad world can be found in Van Fossen's Regents edition and in Eric Rothstein's "Structure as Meaning in *The Jew of Malta*," *JEGP* 65 (1966): 260–73. As Rothstein points out, Spivack, Bevington, and Cole led the way in utilizing morality plays and other elements of the dominant Christian historical background to understand *The Jew* primarily in terms of the conventional moral judgment it brings to bear on Barabas and others throughout. According to this argument, which is fundamentally congruent with Babb's thematic approach and is widely accepted now in place of the earlier view of the play as the aborted tragedy of Barabas, "*The Jew of Malta* is a spectacle of personified evil at work, rather than a spectacle of tragic suffering" (Cole, *Suffering and Evil*, p. 123). The substance of Cole's argument for unified moral vision recurs in Charles G. Masinton's *Christopher Marlowe's Tragic Vision: A Study in Damnation* (Athens: Ohio University Press, 1972) and William L. Godshalk's *The Marlovian World Picture* (The Hague: Mouton, 1974). It should be emphasized that most "moral" readings of the play transform what sometimes used to be seen as an attack on Christianity into a satirical exposure of bad Christians. Alan Dessen speaks for this view in "The Elizabethan Stage Jew and Christian Example: Gerontus, Barabas, and Shylock," *MLQ* 35 (1974): 231–45. Alfred Harbage is the only recent moral conventionalizer, so far as I know, to take the radical step of pronouncing Ferneze a proper Christian hero whose actions "would have been greeted by an Elizabethan audience with warm moral approval" ("Innocent Barabas," *TDR* 8 [1964]: 47–58). On the other hand, Harry Levin, whose book preceded any other study cited in this note, is singular in taking an opposite course toward a coherent view of the play by upholding Barabas as a grand Marlovian "extremist" throughout (*The Overreacher*, p. 75). Though I am at one with all these "unifiers" in accepting the play as an integral whole, the difference between my understanding of it and theirs—especially those who attribute a consistently superior moral judgment to the implied audience—should be clear.

11 I agree with Stephen Greenblatt that we want Barabas to revive and continue to entertain us, but I would not say, as Greenblatt does, that this wish "identifies" us with the Jew: "Marlowe, Marx, and Anti-Semitism," *CritI* 5 (1978): 302–3. Even if one accepts James L. Simmons's argument that Barabas's body is tossed into the playhouse yard here, it needn't follow that the action seals our alliance with him as "Elizabethan young Turks": "Elizabethan Stage Practice and Marlowe's *The Jew of Malta*," *RenD* 4 (1971): 103–4. Greenblatt and Simmons are among the comparatively few

critics who suggest that the audience is engaged with the knavish Barabas. Others who do so include Levin (*The Overreacher*, p. 73), Bawcutt (Revels edition, *Jew of Malta*, p. 26), L. C. Knights (*Further Explorations* [London: Chatto and Windus, 1965], p. 93), T. W. Craik in his introduction to his New Mermaid edition (London: Ernest Benn, 1966, pp. xiii–xv), and Erich Segal ("Marlowe's *Schadenfreude*: Barabas as Comic Hero," in *Veins of Humor,* ed. Harry Levin [Cambridge: Harvard University Press, 1972], pp. 69–91). Of the arguments to this effect, J. B. Steane's, in *Marlowe: A Critical Study* (Cambridge: Cambridge University Press, 1964), is probably the strongest and most thorough. He portrays Barabas as our "entertainer," who keeps us laughing at others with him just as Richard III does (p. 172) and whose masterful personality and lively wit make him a "Volpone and Mosca in one" (p. 186). Naturally, arguments that we are engaged by Barabas's knavery come closer to my own view of him than do those that deplore his loss of tragic stature or place him safely in a moral context; but Steane and those who agree with him about Barabas's entertaining antics tend to treat him as a typically engaging knave, very much like Richard III (Bawcutt and Craik also make this specific comparison). They accurately recognize the kind of character Barabas is and the kind of response such a character normally evokes. *Among* his kind, however, Barabas is exceptionally provoking and uncharacteristically elusive, especially in his unsettling habit of playing tricks on us as well as on the deserving dupes in Malta. That is one reason (together, no doubt, with presuppositions about Marlowe) why critics have on the whole been less readily attracted by his sport than by Richard's.

12 The question of *The Jew*'s relationship to Machiavelli's ideas themselves and to the Elizabethan understanding of them is pursued by Irving Ribner, "Marlowe and Machiavelli," *CL* 6 (1954): 348–56; and N. W. Bawcutt, "Machiavelli and Marlowe's *The Jew of Malta,*" *RenD*, n.s. 3 (1970): 3–49.

13 I would insist on adding this twist to Bawcutt's suggestion that Barabas implicates us as "fellow connoisseurs of villainy" through his address to us here (Revels edition, *Jew of Malta*, p. 31).

14 There are, of course, fewer opportunities to match a reading of this play against a performance than is the case with *Richard III*. In a review article, James L. Smith (taking T. S. Eliot's characterization of *The Jew* as a savage farce for his touchstone) finds that a 1922 production left the harsh bite out of its humor and notes a Reading University production of 1954 as "the first attempt to weave together the play's contradictory elements" ("*The Jew of Malta* in the Theatre," in *Christopher Marlowe*, ed. Brian Morris [London: Ernest Benn, 1968], pp. 1–23). This latter staging sounds as though it aimed at effects closely approximating those suggested in my own analysis. Smith favors even more the black comedy of the 1964 Royal Shakespeare Company production, though his description indicates that this was a case where a director's conception overrode the text by elevating Barabas (several of whose self-damning references to policy were cut) above Ferneze, who was "down-graded into a whimpering weakling" (pp. 19–21). For speculation about the original staging of the play, see Bawcutt's Revels edition, pp. 199–201.

3 Volpone

1 Citations are from Alvin Kernan's edition of *Volpone* in the Yale Ben Jonson (New Haven: Yale University Press, 1962). P. H. Davison's analysis of Volpone in "Old Comedy" terms as both the "deflating Ironical Buffoon" and an "Impostor" suggests the same essential duality as my "chimera of fool and knave": "*Volpone* and the Old Comedy," *MLQ* 24 (1963): 151–57.

2 According to Peter Carlson in "Judging Spectators," *ELH* 44 (1977): 443–57, what Jonson says in and around his plays about audiences constantly reminds us "that we must observe with care and attention." What I argue here is that the very presentation of *Volpone* implies an audience that does so. It should be clear that the process of detachment I describe through my discussion of the opening sequence does not simply depend on the moral judgment that many critics, following the lead of L. C. Knights in *Drama and Society in the Age of Jonson* (London: Chatto and Windus, 1937), insist that Volpone's first speech provokes against him. Readings that emphasize judgment usually also emphasize (as Jonson's own dedicatory Epistle does) the play's "doctrine," so that judgment is steered, in John S. Weld's phrase, by "the moral truisms of the time" ("Christian Comedy: *Volpone*," *SP* 51 [1954]: 172–93). This emphasis naturally suggests kinship with the native English morality drama, a connection that is most fully traced in Alan Dessen's *Jonson's Moral Comedy* (Evanston, Ill.: Northwestern University Press, 1971). Against this dominant critical tendency to take the play "very seriously indeed," as David Cook says we should (*Volpone* [London: Methuen, 1962], p. 27), relatively few have been as absolute in defense of its "hearty laughter" as are Ralph Nash, "The Comic Intent of *Volpone*," *SP* 44 (1947): 26–40; or Rufus Putney, "Jonson's Poetic Comedy," *PQ* 41 (1962): 188–204. Most who appreciate *Volpone*'s humor also see tension between that humor and the play's serious moral intent, often in terms of the divisive pull between theatrical attraction and moral judgment that seems intrinsic to mischievous knaves. Donald Gertmenian and C. N. Manlove describe the friction that many readers sense between judgment and entertainment, arguing that "the source of delight in the play is its most corrupt character" (Gertmenian, "Comic Experience in *Volpone* and *The Alchemist*," *SEL* 17 [1977]: 247–58), that we admire Volpone and Mosca "for reasons that have little to do with morality, in precisely the way that we admire a fine performance" (Manlove, "The Double View in *Volpone*," *SEL* 19 [1979]: 239–52), and that the moral catastrophe is uncomfortably imposed on a play whose delightful knaves have gotten out of control. Countering arguments of pure moral judgment against Volpone, pure delight in him, or irreconcilable tension between these impulses in the play, I try to show how our *comic* judgment (or understanding) distances us from Volpone throughout and is therefore not put on a collision course with the final moral judgment of him, though the *moods* of mirth and doom may in fact clash at the end. My argument that by and large comedy enforces judgment and laughter affirms the values that the play approves could find support in Michael McCanles's "Festival in Jonsonian Comedy," *RenD* 8 (1977): 203–19. McCanles's article

does not focus on *Volpone*, and the play's comparatively stern conclusion might test some of his terms, but his basic thesis that "the capacity for pleasure and festivity" is one of "the operative norms in Jonson's comic vision" would, I believe, still apply: "To the extent that Jonson's plays themselves portray the banishment of perverse festival, the audience participates simultaneously in this banishment and consequently in the true festival which is a Jonson play" (pp. 206, 218).

3   The problematic nature of Mosca's early flattery may be further underscored by contrasting it with a simple model of the same situation in the first act of Plautus's *The Brothers Menaechmus* (in the Penguin Classics edition, *The Pot of Gold and Other Plays*, trans. E. F. Watling [Baltimore: Penguin Books, 1965], pp. 107–8). John Creaser maintains that Volpone and Mosca are playing *to* one another with mutual awareness in these exchanges: "Volpone: The Mortifying of the Fox," *EIC* 25 (1975): 329–56. That is a possible reading, but I would emphasize that we are encouraged to *speculate* about such possibilities as we watch these early sequences.

4   Gail Kern Paster's fine essay, "Ben Jonson's Comedy of Limitation," *SP* 72 (1975): 51–71, notes the constricting nature of Volpone's bedridden role and points out that his successes in the play are limited to the confines of his chamber. Peter Hyland's observation on "Jonson's [or Volpone's] remarkably infrequent use of the 'aside' for comic purposes" in this sequence supports my point about it: *Disguise and Role-Playing in Ben Jonson's Drama* (Salzburg: University of Salzburg, 1977), p. 72. It is also noteworthy that Tyrone Guthrie's productions, trying to give Volpone *command* of our amusement here, had to invent lively (and surely unwarranted) stage-business for him (R. B. Parker, "*Volpone* in Performance: 1921–1972," *RenD* 9 [1978]: 168). Guthrie clearly wanted the actors he directed in the part to take advantage of what Creaser claims to be the "unique rapport with the audience" that Volpone should enjoy, a claim based on the theory that "in the theatre any character who acknowledges that he is acting a part, and relishes it, has a peculiarly strong relation with the audience ("The Mortifying of the Fox," 344–45). This idea, of course, coincides exactly with my general thesis about knavery's theatrical attraction for us. As I am attempting to show, however, several things, including Volpone's self-conscious problems with his knave's role, modify our view in his case—which may be one reason why Guthrie felt compelled to add some textually unjustified "relish" of his own.

5   Mark A. Anderson notes that Mosca's teasing of Volpone's hopes in this scene is of a kind with his teasing of the fools: "Structure and Response in *Volpone*," *RMS* 19 (1975): 47–71. Anderson, like most others who focus on responses to the play (e.g., S. L. Goldberg, "Folly into Crime: The Catastrophe of *Volpone*," *MLQ* 20 [1959]: 233–42), posits a tension between enjoyment and judgment of the knaves that reflects the ambivalence others have seen *in* the play (see note 2). Douglas Duncan resolves what is commonly seen as the knaves' appeal into instructive purpose by arguing that Jonson, in the tradition of Lucian and Erasmus, "teases" his audience, provoking us into "foolish" responses and also prompting the witty among

us to recognize and thereby resist these "delusive sleights," so that the play becomes a test for us (*Ben Jonson and The Lucianic Tradition* [Cambridge: Cambridge University Press, 1979]). James A. Ridell, in "*Volpone's* Fare," *SEL* 21 (1981): 307–18, also has the play confronting its audience in order to separate sheep from goats. Whether divisive responses are seen to be intentional and instructive or confusing and disruptive, theatrical engagement is normally attributed to our pleasure (however dangerous) in the knaves' wit and art, and detachment, when and if it comes, has usually been considered a matter of moral judgment. My argument here departs from this norm to the extent that it analyzes our detachment from Volpone theatrically rather than morally and links our enjoyment of the play with our amused scrutiny of his self-conscious knavery. Some studies suggesting that detachment is in fact a customary effect of Jonson's dramaturgy are: William A. Armstrong, "Ben Jonson and Jacobean Stagecraft," in *Jacobean Theatre*, Stratford-upon-Avon Studies 1, ed. John Russell Brown and Bernard Harris (London: Arnold, 1960), 43–62; Patrick R. Williams, "Ben Jonson's Satiric Choreography," *RenD* 9 (1978): 121–45; and Gabriele Jackson, *Vision and Judgment in Ben Jonson's Drama* (New Haven: Yale University Press, 1968).

6   Jonas Barish urges the "comic justice" of Volpone's discomfiture here ("The Double Plot in *Volpone*," *MP* 51 [1953]: 83–92). Duncan claims that Volpone gains "a kind of comic sympathy" from us as he cowers under Lady Wouldbe's harangue (*Jonson and the Lucianic Tradition*, p. 163). Perhaps in some sense he does, but I would still insist that we laugh *at* his plight and that the comic effect is thus radically different from our engagement with a wittily superior knave.

7   Ian Donaldson attributes to this speech many of the characteristics with which knaves customarily engage us in their soliloquies, including complicity and amused confidentiality: "Volpone: Quick and Dead," *EIC* 21 (1971): 121–34. Though it is of this general kind, the soliloquy's distinctive traits keep us from sharing in Mosca's point of view very fully.

8   Volpone's concoction of his final and fatal scheme is a focal point for differing readings of the play. To argue, as Herford and Simpson and many others do, that Volpone is brought down by his own overconfident audacity is to miss the clear signs of his anxiety about his "fears" as act 5 opens (*Ben Jonson*, ed. C. H. Herford and Percy Simpson [Oxford: The Clarendon Press, 1925–52], 2:59). And even some readings that are more in tune with the play than this one is still tend to accept at face value Volpone's assertion that he enjoyed Mosca's "masterpiece" more than he would have enjoyed Celia herself, whereas the context plainly indicates that this is a face-saving cover-up (as he has just said privately, he did *not* enjoy the public trial scene, and Mosca is pushing him to expose that weakness here): see, for example, Nash, "The Comic Intent of *Volpone*"; Alexander Leggatt, "The Suicide of Volpone," *UTQ* 39 (1969): 19–32; and Stephen Greenblatt, "The False Ending in *Volpone*," *JEGP* 75 (1976): 90–104. Creaser correctly notes, against the argument of overconfidence, that "Volpone begins the fifth act

daunted and anxious, not 'exulting and daring' ": "The Mortifying of the Fox," p. 346. And J. B. Bamborough remarks that Volpone depends here on his knavish mischief "almost like a drug": *Ben Jonson* (London: Hutchinson, 1970), pp. 86–87.

9 Some readers understand Volpone to be referring to Lady Pol here, since the knaves had been mocking her a few lines earlier. But could he be delighted by the thought that *she* might love him? More likely, Volpone moves from Mosca's "her grace, her youth, her beauty" to thoughts of Celia. Mosca, in fact, may not follow that leap and may still refer to Lady Pol in his response; but Volpone's "Dost thou say so?" surely echoes his earlier hopes about Celia. If he has taken to flattering himself with such thoughts about the insufferable Lady Pol, he is undergoing an even more demeaning comedown here than my reading supposes.

10 Duncan notes "the vulnerability of the overviewer" when Volpone watches Mosca torment the bilked "heirs": *Jonson and the Lucianic Tradition*, p. 153.

11 Hence the tension felt in the play by critics cited in earlier notes. For older readings of *Volpone* that make it sound like a lurid tragedy (the essay in the Herford and Simpson edition, for example) and some more recent ones that insist on its tough, ironic realism, the conclusion can seem both grim *and* appropriate. According to Lawrence L. Levin, "Jonson is saying, in effect, that in dealing with realistic problems in society he refuses to give a fairy-tale ending and cheerfully dispel the provocative and disturbing fruits of his labors" ("Justice and Society in *Sejanus* and *Volpone*," *Discourse* 13 [1970]: 319–24). Others who match or surpass Levin in their dark accounts of the play include Edward B. Partridge, *The Broken Compass: A Study of the Major Comedies of Ben Jonson* (London: Chatto and Windus, 1958); Richard A. Dutton, "*Volpone* and *The Alchemist*: A Comparison in Satiric Techniques," *RMS* 18 (1974): 36–62; and George A. E. Parfitt, "Volpone," *EIC* 21 (1971): 411–12, and "Virtue and Pessimism in Three Plays by Ben Jonson," *SlitI* 6 (1973): 23–40. Emphasizing the gullibility or corruptibility of the avocatori who pass such severe judgment on Volpone makes the conclusion even more harshly ironic, of course. Bleak readings of the play are given a kind of back-handed support by adaptations that alter the text in order to "brighten" or "soften" it for production, and such alterations characteristically make the conclusion more conventionally "comic" (see David McPherson, "Rough Beast into Tame Fox: The Adaptations of *Volpone*," *SlitI* 6 [1973]: 77–84). Others who argue, as I do, that Jonson's own text gives Volpone a measure of comic triumph over stern moral and legal judgment at the end include Robert E. Knoll, *Ben Jonson's Plays: An Introduction* (Lincoln: University of Nebraska Press, 1964), p. 92; William Empson, "Volpone," *HudR* 21 (1968–69): 651–66; Leggatt, "The Suicide of Volpone," 30–31; and Creaser, "The Mortifying of the Fox," 350–53.

4 Vindice

1 *Hamlet*, 5.2.370–74. Citations from *The Revenger's Tragedy* are from Lawrence J. Ross's edition in the Regents Renaissance Drama Series (Lincoln: University of Nebraska Press, 1966).

2 My characterization of Vindice obviously differs radically from the older view of him as a "repulsively morbid" villain (Clarence V. Boyer, *The Villain as Hero in Elizabethan Tragedy* [London: Routledge, 1914], pp. 148–52) and, perhaps even more significantly, from the more recent consensus that he is subjected to our moral judgment through the course of the play. According to most versions of the moral reading, which largely replaced earlier accounts of *The Revenger's Tragedy* as a fin-de-siècle horror show or neurotic nightmare, Vindice "deteriorates steadily throughout the play" as he pursues his vengeance and thereby sinks to the level of the vicious court he attacks (Henry Hitch Adams, "Cyril Tourneur on Revenge," *JEGP* 48 [1949]: 72–87). Since I argue for increasing theatrical engagement with Vindice, nowhere are the different results of my approach from the application of "objective" moral judgment more striking than in this case. Others who advance the "moral deterioration" thesis (with whatever variations) include Alvin Kernan, *The Cankered Muse: Satire of the English Renaissance* (New Haven: Yale University Press, 1959); Irving Ribner, *Jacobean Tragedy: The Quest for Moral Order* (London: Methuen, 1962); Peter Murray, *A Study of Cyril Tourneur* (Philadelphia: University of Pennsylvania Press, 1964); Ross, in the introduction to the Regents edition I use here; J. L. Simmons, "The Tongue and Its Office in *The Revenger's Tragedy*," *PMLA* 92 (1977): 56–68; and Charles A. and Elaine S. Hallett, who trace "Vindice's progressive deterioration" through "three stages" in *The Revenger's Madness: A Study of Revenge Tragedy Motifs* (Lincoln: University of Nebraska Press, 1980). R. A. Foakes, in his Revels edition of *The Revenger's Tragedy* (Cambridge: Harvard University Press, 1966), departs from this emphasis on degeneration by accusing Vindice of being "contaminated by what he condemns" from the very beginning. I remarked in my introduction that critics find it harder to acknowledge engagement with the professedly moral Vindice than with the villainous Richard; it is especially noteworthy, I think, that Foakes cites Vindice's pleasure in "his own cunning intrigues," his "rejoicing in his skill," as evidence in the judgment *against* him. Whereas such phrases are customarily used to explain the theatrical attractiveness of out-and-out knaves such as Richard or Volpone, they are almost always used to condemn Vindice on moral grounds. Recent critics who have resisted the uplifting moral trend and who still find *The Revenger's Tragedy* dark or disturbing include B. J. Layman, "Tourneur's Artificial Noon: The Design of *The Revenger's Tragedy*," *MLQ* 34 (1973): 20–35; Ronald Huebert, "*The Revenger's Tragedy* and the Fallacy of the Excluded Middle," *UTQ* 48 (1978): 10–22; and Nicholas Brooke, *Horrid Laughter in Jacobean Tragedy* (Totowa, N. J.: Barnes and Noble, 1979).

3 In Richard's world time's effects, if not always pretty, are at least portrayed

as reassuringly normal: "So now prosperity begins to mellow / And drop into the rotten mouth of death" (4.4.1–2).

4 See Kernan's discussion of Vindice as a satirist in *The Cankered Muse,* pp. 221–32. For Michael E. Mooney, the satirist is one of Vindice's three personas (" 'This Luxurious Circle': *Figurenposition* in *The Revenger's Tragedy,*" *ELR* 13 [1983]: 162–81).

5 This fundamental theatrical distinction between our experience of Vindice and of other revengers in the play is generally overlooked by readers who emphasize thematic parallels among them and level moral judgment against them all alike.

6 Fredson Bowers notes that Vindice tends to get "lost in the maze" of villainous intrigues at court, but sees that fact (as I do not) as a dramatic flaw, since the play "lacks on occasion a controlling protagonist." See *Elizabethan Revenge Tragedy* (Princeton: Princeton University Press, 1940), p. 136.

7 Philip J. Ayres notes the parallels between Vindice's schemes and those of the Duchess's sons and argues that the latter, by burlesquing Vindice, reduce him to their level in our eyes. That seems to me a "reductive" reading indeed. See "Parallel Action and Reductive Technique in *The Revenger's Tragedy,*" *ELN* 8 (1970): 103–7, and *Tourneur: The Revenger's Tragedy* (London: Edward Anrold, 1977), pp. 34–35.

8 Readings that focus on the theatricalism of Vindice's "performance" here and throughout the play are becoming dominant in critical studies of *The Revenger's Tragedy,* which is now often seen as a play about revenge plays (Leslie Sanders, "*The Revenger's Tragedy*: A Play on the Revenge Play," *Ren&R* 10 [1974]: 25–36), or about *Hamlet* (Howard Felperin, *Shakespearean Representation: Mimesis and Modernity in Elizabethan Tragedy* [Princeton: Princeton University Press, 1977]), or about theater itself (Scott McMillin, "Acting and Violence: *The Revenger's Tragedy* and Its Departures from *Hamlet,*" *SEL* 24 [1984]: 275–91). See also Howard Pearce, "*Virtù* and *Poesis* in *The Revenger's Tragedy,*" *ELH* 43 (1976): 10–37; and Lillian Wilds, "The Revenger as Dramatist: A Study of the Character-as-Dramatist in *The Revenger's Tragedy,*" *BRMMLA* 30 (1976): 113–22. Vindice's flair for dramatics is not necessarily seen as an engaging trait in theatricalist studies and is sometimes held against him (Felperin, *Shakespearean Representation,* pp. 166–69) in a way that recalls primarily moral assessments (see note 2); but Mooney has the audience participating "with Vindice in the performance of the revenger's tragedy" ("*Figurenposition* in *The Revenger's Tragedy,*" p. 181), and Richard T. Brucher closely approximates my own analysis of theatrical engagement with Vindice in the second half of the play ("Fantasies of Violence: *Hamlet* and *The Revenger's Tragedy,*" *SEL* 21 [1981]: 257–70). Brucher, however, emphasizes the audience's own "fantasies about power, control, and poetic justice in a corrupt world," and argues that *The Revenger's Tragedy* plays *to* these fantasies and indulges them (as the Dirty Harry movies do), whereas *Hamlet* brings them *into* play and then places them in the context of life's meaning and value. R. F. Foakes makes a similar invidious comparison with a similar stress on the "art" of violence,

but between Hamlet and Vindice rather than between the two plays, since Foakes agrees with the moralists that *The Revenger's Tragedy* places and condemns Vindice's own pleasure in his crafty cruelty ("The Art of Cruelty: Hamlet and Vindice," *ShS* 26 [1973]: 21–31).

9 For a less familiar but useful contrast, see *The Tragedy of Hoffman* (act 3, scene 1), in which the innocent victims play to us with straight pathos, and nothing in Hoffman's management of the scene prompts us to follow his bidding to Lorrique: "Helpe me to sing a hymne unto the fates / Compos'd of laughing interjections" (Tudor Facsimile Text, ed. John S. Farmer [London, 1913]). Maurice Charney's account of Vindice's murder of the Duke suggests that its effects are too complex to place simply within either the "moral" or "esthetic" categories he identifies in "The Persuasiveness of Violence in Elizabethan Plays," *RenD* n.s. 2 (1969): 59–70.

10 Jonas Barish makes the surprisingly rare observation that the play distinguishes Vindice and Hippolito favorably from the ducal family in these sequences. See "The True and False Families of *The Revenger's Tragedy*," in *English Renaissance Drama: Essays in Honor of Madeleine Doran and Mark Eccles,* ed. Standish Henning, Robert Kimbrough, and Richard Knowles (Carbondale: Southern Illinois University Press, 1976), pp. 142–54.

11 T. W. Craik points out the apparent approval of heaven here, which readers anxious to condemn Vindice on moral grounds (or to argue that the play does so) frequently ignore. See "*The Revenger's Tragedy*," *EIC* 6 (1956): 482–83. In " 'There It Goes' — or Does It?: Thunder in *The Revenger's Tragedy* and a Catch-Phrase in Shakespeare, Marlowe, and Middleton," *ELN* 13 (1975): 6–10, Daniel J. Jacobson questions the authenticity of the common editorial insertion of a thunderclap into Vindice's speech at 4.2.194 (I use Ross's line numbers here). But there can be no question about the thunder that evidently applauds the revengers in 5.3.41 ff.

12 Critics differ radically in their readings of Antonio. But both those who say that he restores or enforces the proper moral perspective (e.g., Bowers, *Elizabethan Revenge Tragedy*, and Kernan, *Cankered Muse*) and those who see him as a cynical contriver who wins this final round from Vindice (as does Pearce, "*Virtù* and *Poesis* in *The Revenger's Tragedy*) credit him, I believe, with more control over the play and our view of it than he actually earns.

13 Among those who note the dramatically winning tone of Vindice's exit speech are Pearce, "*Virtù* and *Poesis*," 35; John Creaser, who likens Vindice's final jaunty resignation to Volpone's, "Volpone: The Mortifying of the Fox," *EIC* 25 (1975): 351; Brian Gibbons, in the introduction to his edition of *The Revenger's Tragedy* (New York: Hill and Wang, 1967), p. xxvi; Barish, "True and False Families," pp. 152–53; and Mooney, "*Figurenposition* in *The Revenger's Tragedy*," 177. Pearce, Mooney, and McMillin ("Acting and Violence") observe that Vindice misappropriates the "knavish sentence" to himself (as Piato) from an attendant noble, who spoke it (not at all knavishly) in 5.1.146–47.

14 Arguments about Vindice's relationship with the audience do not usually have much firsthand experience of performances from which to work.

Stanley Wells's review of the 1966, 1967, and 1969 Royal Shakespeare Company productions, however, suggests that Ian Richardson played up the comic aspects of Vindice's role to the audience in a way that would generally support my thesis ("*The Revenger's Tragedy* Revived," in *Elizabethan Theatre VI,* ed. G. R. Hibbard [Hamden, Conn.: Shoe String Press, 1977], pp. 105–33). Even more telling for my attempt to show how the performed play should direct an audience's responses toward engagement with Vindice (and with specific reference to his winning final exit) is the difference that J. R. Lever acknowledges between his considered moral analysis as a reader and his theatrical experience. He first objectively assesses the "ambivalence" of Vindice's "moral position": "His oscillations between passionate diatribes against vice and joyous participation in the intrigues of court, between laments for his lost mistress and trite aphorisms on women's follies, between Hamlet-like meditations on the vanity of life and sadistic enactments of murder, make him the villain as well as the hero of his own play" (*The Tragedy of State* [London: Methuen, 1971], pp. 32–33). But having thus dissected him, Lever then admits, on the basis of attending the RSC productions, that such measured judgment may evaporate in the theater; that Vindice wins the audience in the way that the "well-loved" Vice used to do or the outlaw still does; and that he "goes unrepentant to his execution, justified in his own eyes, and undoubtedly in the eyes of the audience." That last phrase aptly suggests the alignment between our point of view and Vindice's that I have traced here. My own first opportunity to see the play came at the 1984 Oregon Shakespearean Festival in Ashland, after this manuscript was completed. Despite a curious rearrangement that opened the play with Antonio discovering his dead wife to "certain Lords" (act 1, scene 4), moved to the Youngest Son's trial (act 1, scene 2), and thereby muted Vindice's initial hold on our point of view by placing his introductory soliloquy at the beginning of a third scene, the audience enjoyed the play's bitter humor largely through Vindice from his first appearance to the very end.

15 Like Mooney, but without anticipating his thesis about Vindice's distinct personas and their relationship to *platea* and *locus*, Gibbons notes the presence of such "abrupt shifts" in the play's dialogue (introduction to his edition, p. xvi); and Coburn Freer raises the same question I do about Vindice's shift at this point (*The Poetics of Jacobean Drama* [Baltimore: Johns Hopkins University Press, 1981], p. 85). Freer squeezes too hard on certain passages, I believe, to force his argument that Vindice's behavior (verbal and otherwise) stems from the suspicion that he is actually another illegitimate son of the Duke. Nonetheless, Freer's acute description of Vindice's verbal progress—his failure to control his verse in the first part of the play, his greater control of it as he carries out the murder of the Duke, his subsidence into comic prose and quips thereafter, and his comic control of his final speech—would support my account of Vindice's development as a knave very nicely.

16 Several critics identify the skull as the central image or symbol in the play, though not with the same point in mind about Vindice's understanding of it

that I am making here. See, for example, Kernan, *Cankered Muse*, p. 227; Ross edition, p. xxvii; Ribner, *Jacobean Tragedy,* pp. 82–83; and Murray, *Cyril Tourneur*, p. 193. Richard W. Hillman does remark on the detachment afforded Vindice by his "alliance" with death, though in darker terms than I use here, in "Meaning and Mortality in some Renaissance Revenge Plays," *UTQ* 49 (1979): 1–17.

Index

Adams, Henry Hitch, 170 n.2
Adelman, Janet, 156 nn. 11 and 13
Anderson, Mark A., 167 n. 5
Anti-Semitism: in *The Jew of Malta*, 8, 66–69, 79–84
Asides: effect on point of view, 4–5, 10–11
Awareness, hierarchies and levels of, 4–5, 152

Babb, Howard, 164 n.10
Barber, C. L., 12
Beaumont, Francis, *The Knight of the Burning Pestle*, 3
Beckett, Samuel, *Waiting for Godot*, 152
Bedford, Brian, 158 n.36
Berry, Ralph, 159 n.4
Booth, Stephen, 156 n.11
Bowers, Fredson, 155 n.2
Brooke, C. F. Tucker, 163 n.8
Brooke, Nicholas, 159 n.2
Brucher, Richard T., 171 n.8

Carlson, Peter, 166 n.2
Castle of Perseverance, The, 14
Champion, Larry S., 159 n.2
Cibber, Colley, 158 n.37, 160 n.7
Cole, Douglas, 23, 164 n.10
Complicity: with morality play Vice, 14–15

Confidentiality: effect on point of view, 10–11
Critical approaches: moral, 20–23, 170 n.2; reflective analysis, 22–23; thematic, 20–23, 164 n.10. *See also* Point of view

Detachment, theatrical: and point of view, 4–11
Dramatic perspective, 2–4, 21, 23; multiple, 150–51
Duncan, Douglas, 167 n.5

Empathy, 5–6
Engagement, theatrical: and point of view, 4–11
Evans, Bertrand, 155 n.3

Foakes, R. A., 170 n.2
Freer, Coburn, 173 n.15
French, A. L., 22
Freud, Sigmund, 24
Fulwell, Ulpian: *Like Will to Like*, 12–14, 17, 18–19, 64

Gammer Gurton's Needle, 5, 9, 149–50
Gosson, Stephen: *Plays Confuted in Five Actions*, 156 n.14
Greenblatt, Stephen, 164 n.11
Grotesqueness: characteristic of knaves, 5–6; characteristic of Richard, 32

164 n.11; in relation to *The Revenger's Tragedy*, 123–28, 131–32, 136–38, 145, 170 n.2; in relation to *Volpone*, 99–104, 108, 111, 113–14, 115
Richardson, Ian, 172 n.14
Righter, Anne, 159 n.4
Rossiter, A. P., 159 n.4
Rothstein, Eric, 164 n.10

Sanders, Wilbur, 22
Scholes, Robert, 2
Self-consciousness: in audience response, 13, 17–18, 20, 29–30, 160 n.5
Sen Gupta, S. C., 160 n.8, 161 n.14
Shakespeare, William: *Antony and Cleopatra*, 151; *Hamlet*, 24; *King Lear*, 2–3, 137, 152; *Love's Labor's Lost*, 4; *Measure for Measure*, 150; *The Merry Wives of Windsor*, 9; *A Midsummer Night's Dream*, 9; *Othello*, 152; *The Tempest*, 150; *The Two Gentlemen of Verona*, 18–19. See also *Richard III*
Sheriff, William E., 161 n.14
Simmons, James L., 164 n.11
Smith, James L., 165 n.14
Soellner, Rolf, 156 n.12
Soliloquies: effect on point of view, 4–5, 10–11
Sport: characteristic of knavery, 7, 9
Sprague, Arthur Colby, 158 n.37
Steane, J. B., 164 n.11
Sympathy, 5

Theatricalism: in Renaissance drama, 17, 19–20; in modern drama, 151–52
Tillyard, E. M. W., 21, 160 n.8
Tourneur, Cyril. See *The Revenger's Tragedy*
Tragedy of Hoffman, The, 172 n.9
Trial of Treasure, The, 17

Udall, Nicholas: *Ralph Roister Doister*, 9, 149–50

Van Laan, Thomas, 159 n.4
Vice, the, 11–18, 149; in relation to *The Jew of Malta*, 64, 84, 163 n.7; in relation to *The Revenger's Tragedy*, 172 n.14; in relation to *Richard III*, 29–30, 49

Vickers, Brian, 155 n.4
Volpone, 99–121; illustrating critical approach, 7, 10, 17, 152; in relation to *The Jew of Malta*, 83; in relation to *The Revenger's Tragedy*, 127, 132, 144, 172 n.13

Webster, John: *The Duchess of Malfi*, 151; *The White Devil*, 151
Weimann, Robert, 18–20
Whitaker, Virgil K., 21
Wilson, F. P., 163 n.8
Wit: characteristic of knavery, 7, 9

Library of Congress Cataloging-in-Publication Data
Jones, Robert C., 1936–
Engagement with knavery.
Bibliography: p.
Includes index.
1. English drama (Tragedy)—History and criticism.
2. English drama—Early modern and Elizabethan, 1500–
1600—History and criticism. 3. English drama—17th
century—History and criticism. 4. Point of view
(Literature) 5. Villains in literature. I. Title.
PR658.T7J6 1986 822'.3'09 85-20547
ISBN 0-8223-0520-8